Suzanne Tise-Isoré
Style & Design Collection

TEXT ADVISER
Karine Huguenaud

EDITORIAL COORDINATION
Lara Lo Calzo

GRAPHIC DESIGN
Bernard Lagacé

TRANSLATION FROM THE FRENCH
Barbara Mellor

COPY EDITING AND PROOFREADING
Lindsay Porter

PRODUCTION
Élodie Conjat

COLOR SEPARATION
Les Artisans du Regard, Paris

Printed in Italy by Musumeci

Simultaneously published in French
as *Venise, Invitation privée*.
© Flammarion S.A., Paris, 2022

English-language edition
© Flammarion S.A., Paris, 2022

Flammarion S.A.
87, quai Panhard-et-Levassor
75647 Paris cedex 13
editions.flammarion.com
@styleetdesign-flammarion.com

22 23 24 3 2 1
ISBN: 978-2-08-026216-5
Legal Deposit: 10/2022

FRONT COVER
A table laid in one of the *liagò*
on the piano nobile of
the Palazzo Falier. One of the
oldest palazzi on the Grand
Canal, dating from the
fourteenth century, the
Palazzo Falier has preserved
its historic character and
typically Venetian spirit
while also adapting to the
demands of modern times
and family life.

ENDPAPERS
Mosaic with a fish, detail
from one of the bathrooms
in the Palazzo Falier.

FRONT ENDPAPERS, VERSO
Detail of a *finestra a rui*,
a traditional and typically
Venetian leaded window
design composed of *cives*,
or colored glass discs:
a centuries-old technique
revisited by Marino Barovier,
descendant of one of the
most illustrious and ancient
dynasties of Murano
glassmakers.

PAGE 1
Carved wooden doors
in the Benedetto Marcello
Conservatory of Music.

VENICE
A Private Invitation

text **Servane Giol**   photography **Mattia Aquila**
foreword **Pierre Rosenberg**, Académie Française

Flammarion

CONTENTS

9   Foreword
    ALMOST AS BEAUTIFUL AS VENICE
    Pierre Rosenberg, Académie Française

10 VENICE OF THE VENETIANS: A LIFE EXTRAORDINARY
    Servane Giol

12 LIVING THE EXTRAORDINARY

14 VENETIAN BEAUTY
60 ENTERTAINING, VENETIAN STYLE
70 VENETIAN FESTIVALS AND CELEBRATIONS
86 THE DECORATIVE ARTS IN VENICE

128 MONOPOLIES ON THE EXTRAORDINARY

130 MIRRORS
159 GLASS
194 FABRIC AND LACE
234 CERAMICS AND PORCELAIN
245 STUCCO

256 IN PURSUIT OF THE EXTRAORDINARY

258 THE BIENNALE
263 ARCHITECTS AND INTERIOR DESIGNERS
272 PAINTERS AND SCULPTORS
289 COLLECTORS
290 SECRET GARDENS

304 Acknowledgments
304 Photographic Credits

PAGE 4
Giovanni Giol, President of the Benedetto Marcello Conservatory of Music, with his wife, Servane, on the arcaded loggia that divides the two inner courtyards of the Palazzo Pisani: a setting of peerless Venetian grandeur.

PAGE 5
Giovanni and Servane Giol approaching their home, the Palazzo Falier, along the Grand Canal.

FACING PAGE
The Palazzo Falier, near the Accademia Bridge, is famous for its twin *liagò*, projecting loggias that are exposed to the light on three sides through large windows fitted with tinted glass panes to filter the sun.

ALMOST AS BEAUTIFUL AS VENICE

PIERRE ROSENBERG, Académie Française

"It's almost as beautiful as Venice," exclaimed a young Venetian visitor to Paris, as a *bateau-mouche* glided past on the Seine.

What is there that is *almost* as beautiful as Venice? This is the question that Servane Giol sets out to explore—and in her own way.

She shows us the creations of Venice, not only from the past but also—and too often overlooked—from today: Murano glass, of course (under so much threat now from soaring gas prices), but also mosaics, fabrics, and a whole range of the relatively unsung crafts that have been the glory of Venice in the past and that remain so today. She shows us a living, vibrant Venice, a Venice that is still a home, a Venice that she knows like the back of her hand—and perhaps all the more so for herself being a Venetian, (if only) by adoption. She pays tribute to an *art de vivre* shaped by the city's unique geography, lapped by waters on all sides—not just the Grand Canal but also and especially the lagoon—which isolate the city and oblige those who live there to adapt their way of life accordingly.

Of course the word that matters most is that *almost*—a sigh, a cry from the heart. Mattia Aquila's photographs, grouped so skillfully by Servane Giol, are here to complement and enrich that sigh, to delight and surprise even the most seasoned of aficionados who think they know the city by heart.

That *almost* is at once reassuring and disturbing—but for how much longer.

VENICE OF THE VENETIANS
A LIFE EXTRAORDINARY

SERVANE GIOL

Whenever I tell people my address, their response—wide-eyed, astonished—is always the same: "You live in Venice? Do people still live there? Do Venetians still exist?" Venice exerts its own fascination over us, but perhaps its real mystery lies, even more than in the city itself, in its inhabitants. It is true that its population is shrinking with every passing year. As early as 1902, Maurice Barrès observed: "There are no Venetians anymore. The real population of Venice seems to be made up of cosmopolitans, millionaires, and artists, confined largely within the old historic palazzi and surveyed by incessant processions of tourists." So the problem is not a new one.

The surprise generated by my address is not due solely to the declining numbers of Venetians, nor to the articles in the press that have long been prophesying doom for the city on its lagoon. What it's really about is how people manage to live in Venice—that special Venetian *art de vivre*, or the idea that we have of it. This magical city, this city without cars, seems impossible. Its geography, its inconvenience, and its lack of modern comforts seem to make everything so complicated: shopping, raising children, and—especially—living in its palazzi. For however open Venice may seem to the foreign visitor, gaining access to its private residences, a little-known and remarkable world, remains difficult.

As a great connoisseur of the city, French novelist Jean d'Ormesson was emphatic in his belief that Venetians "elude all norms and classifications. One cannot live in an exceptional city without becoming, in consequence, somewhat exceptional oneself." It is this "exceptional" quality that I seek to share in this book. And what better way of understanding it than through enticing glimpses of the way of life of Venetians within the intimacy of the palazzi that are still private residences, most of which have never been photographed before?

Jean Giono reminds us pertinently that "tourists have turned this city into a stage set for the use of tourists ... if we are not conscious of the fact that it is first and foremost a city for the use of Venetians, then we scarcely see it at all." The Venetians seem to have pulled off a miracle, somehow carrying on with their lives while remaining unseen by the rest of the world and the throngs of visitors that pour into their city every day—and retaining all their mystery as they do so. This book is my invitation to you to meet them and, along the way, to discover intriguing figures who are often neglected in our collective memory, in favor of more celebrated visitors who were merely passing through.

Research in the Arrivabene and Frigerio Zeno private archives has lifted the veil to reveal some aspects of the way life was lived in these wonderful palazzi in the twentieth century, providing glimpses of an art of entertaining that was inextricably linked with Venetian artisans and their creations. This art of entertaining is still enjoyed today, and is celebrated here in tables dressed specially for us by the owners who welcome us into their homes. For the Venice I know is lived in, vibrant, special—and this is the Venice that I want to share with you in these pages.

Here you will find a fresh approach to all that the Venetians excel in, from their art of entertaining, to their decorative arts, their festivities, and their music. The Serenissima's palazzi are the setting, while the décor is provided by her arts and crafts. Mirrors, glass, gold thread, lace—extraordinary materials with evocative names, all of them Venetian monopolies, which, though they may now be obsolete, are forever inseparable from the city on the lagoon and its artists and artisans, synonymous for centuries with talent, inventiveness, and creativity.

Montesquieu described the Venetians as "the finest people in the world," perhaps because they are constantly evolving. New generations of designers, artists, architects, writers, decorators, and collectors have chosen to make Venice their home. Together they bring a breath of fresh air and inspiration, and one that will safeguard the city's unique craftsmanship.

FACING PAGE
Servane Giol at home, on one of the *liagò* of the Palazzo Falier. A Venetian by adoption for over twenty years, Servane invites us to discover a unique art of living in the privacy of palazzi that are still lived in.

LIVING
THE EXTRAORDINARY

VENETIAN BEAUTY

VENETIAN BLONDES

While it may be so famous that it has given its name to a color, there was nothing natural about the strawberry blonde shade so beloved of Venetian blondes. According to legend, elegant ladies would clamber up on to their *altane,* the wooden deck structures perched on the roofs of their palazzi, and bleach their hair in the sun, sheltering beneath broad-brimmed hats with the crown removed. Recipes varied for the bleaching paste that they used, but probably one of the most effective formulae was transcribed by Giovanni Marinello in *Gli ornamenti delle donne*, a collection of beauty secrets published in Venice in 1574. Drawing on Graeco-Roman and Arabic traditions, this recommended taking "a good measure of the soap water used to bleach silk; boil this with a little alum for about the time it takes to say a *Paternoster*. Then add two ounces of burnt lead and leave it all to boil until a piece of white cloth dipped in it turns black. Leave to cool. Finally, pour into a glass bottle. Add two ounces of powdered Damascus soap and keep in the sun ... bathe the hair with a sponge soaked in this excellent mixture, and in under an hour it will become as blonde as gold threads. If you prefer red hair, do not dry it completely in the sun."

Venetian blondeness, whether natural or fake, provided inspiration to a litany of painters and poets. "The beauty of Venetian women has generally been better portrayed by painters than by writers," noted Jean d'Ormesson. Even Cleopatra was blonde, as depicted by Tiepolo in the Palazzo Labia in the mid-eighteenth century (in the image of Maria Labia, mistress of the house).

One of the most famous of Venetian folk songs features a blonde beauty. *La Biondina in Gondoleta* was composed by the poet Antonio Lamberti in 1788, in honor of Contessa Marina Querini Benzoni, a beautiful patrician woman loved by Byron, admired by Stendhal, and sculpted by Canova. In *Italia*, his account of his trip to Italy published in 1852, Théophile Gautier marveled at the fact that the song had become the model for barcarolles sung by Venetian gondoliers, to the point of being cited by Rossini in the singing lesson in *The Barber of Seville*. Gautier offered a translation of the subtle Venetian dialect: "A pretty blonde got into a gondola and the poor little thing fell asleep in the boat, slumbering with delight on the arm of the gondolier, who woke her from time to time, but the rocking of the gondola soon sent the beautiful child back to sleep ... But who could find rest with passion at his side? In the end, annoyed by this interminable sleep, *il fait de l'insolent*, and has no reason to regret it. ' Oh heavens!' he cries in his naive vanity, 'what beautiful things she said, and I did! Never in my life or in all my days have I been so happy.'"

PAGE 12
Detail of a painted chinoiserie decoration in an anteroom of the Palazzo Papadopoli.

PAGE 13
Seaside fun and games on the beach of the Grand Hôtel des Bains on the Lido in the 1920s (Frigerio Zeno private archive).

FACING PAGE
Portrait of a "Venetian blonde," an eighteenth-century painting mounted in the nineteenth as a dessus-de-porte in the Tapestry Room of the Palazzo Papadopoli.

PAGE 16
Belle Époque photographic portraits of society ladies and children, including that of the Italian queen, Margherita of Savoy (Frigerio Zeno private archive).

PAGE 17
A selection of dance-card holders from the collection of Contessa Frigerio Zeno, exquisite testimonies to the parties and balls that punctuated the Venetian social scene.

A CENTURY OF VENETIAN BEAUTY: THE ARRIVABENE SISTERS

No meditation on the beauty of Venetian women could fail to mention the four generations of the Arrivabene women, beautiful, free, and proud of their Venetian identity. Today, as in the past, the Arrivabene sisters light up Venetian life with their elegance.

It all began in 1900, at the dawn of the new century, when Vera Papadopoli Aldobrandini married Count Giberto Arrivabene Valenti Gonzaga, from a noble Mantuan family. The daughter of a wealthy banker of Greek origin, Vera inherited the magnificent Palazzo Papadopoli on the Grand Canal near San Polo. Her beauty and that of her sister Maddalena were celebrated not only by painters—Umberto Brunelleschi and Vittorio Matteo Corcos painted their respective portraits—but also by poets such as Gabriele D'Annunzio, who presented her with a youthful photograph of himself with the bold dedication: "To Contessa Vera this image of an adolescent long ago who would have killed himself for her eyes." The many portraits of Vera form a rare and eloquent testimony not only to her beauty but also to the art of living in Venice in the twentieth century. The Arrivabene family has preserved an exceptional collection from this period, testifying to the whirl of balls, operas, costume galas, and strolls in St. Mark's Square that formed the gentle currency of daily life for an element of the Venetian elite.

Vera's two daughters, Nicoletta and Maddalena Arrivabene, born in 1905 and 1906, breathed new life into Venetian high society when they made their debut in the 1920s. In the presence of the old guard—Annina Morosini, Princess of San Faustino, the Mocenigos, the Treves, and Vittorio and Lyda Cini—memorable gala evenings at the Palazzo Papadopoli, the first since the end of World War I and the death of Count Giberto, heralded the dawn of a new Venetian golden age.

The 1920s and 1930s in Venice were an era of fabled splendor. According to Paul Morand, Venice was the "most brilliant city in Europe," a magnet for members of a cosmopolitan high society attracted, largely thanks to Elsa Maxwell, by the opening of the Grand Hôtel des Bains and the Hotel Excelsior on the Lido, and by Count Giuseppe Volpi's founding of the Venice Film Festival.

Nicoletta and Maddalena Arrivabene, nicknamed Niki and Madina, were the queens who reigned over this perpetual whirl of parties, dressed as an odalisque or a Javanese beauty at the Oriental Ball given by Volpi; dancing among the beach cabins of the Lido with Serge Lifar in the era of Diaghilev's Ballets Russes; and wearing the creations of Jean Patou, who designed Niki's wedding gown.

The two sisters were to marry two brothers: two of the Visconti brothers, the third of whom was later to direct the cinematic masterpiece *Death in Venice*. Both weddings were celebrated amid the opulence of St. Mark's Basilica. More recently, in 2021, another Arrivabene beauty traveled to her wedding by gondola from the Palazzo Papadopoli, when Vera Arrivabene married Count Briano Martinoni, a descendant of the Viscontis, at the church of San Pantalon—and so things come full circle.

Today, Giberto and Bianca Arrivabene still live in the Palazzo Papadopoli with their son, Leonardo, and their four dazzling daughters, Viola, Vera, Mafalda, and Maddalena. The eldest sisters, Viola and Vera, now seek to promote Venetian excellence through their own brand of velvet slippers, ViBi Venezia. Having inherited their ancestors' exquisite taste for fashion and celebrations, they are the perfect embodiment of a new creative generation in Venice.

PAGES 20–21 AND BELOW
Photographs of the wedding of Maddalena Arrivabene Valenti Gonzaga, known as Madina, to Luigi Visconti di Modrone, on April 24, 1929: leaving the Palazzo Papadopoli in a gondola and the procession across St. Mark's Square, where a throng of curious onlookers gathered to watch the spectacle (Arrivabene private archive).

FACING PAGE
Madina Arrivabene, photographed around 1930 in a white georgette dress by Jean Patou and a set of art deco Bulgari jewelry. Jean Patou also designed the bridal gown for Niki's wedding in St. Mark's Basilica the following year.

ABOVE
Like her grandmothers,
Niki and Madina,
Vera Arrivabene traveled by
gondola from the Palazzo
Papadopoli for her marriage
to Count Briano Martinoni
on October 16, 2021.
FACING PAGE
The ceremony in the
church of San Pantalon
in Dorsoduro.

A DYNASTY OF VENETIAN ARTISTS

Like Veronese, Titian, and Tiepolo in their era, later artists celebrated the beauties of Venice in the nineteenth and twentieth centuries. The Accademia di Belle Arti thus saw three of its students shine at Biennales: Ettore Tito, Guglielmo Ciardi, and Luigi Nono. Their favored subjects, mostly local women observed in the simplicity of a daily life far removed from the splendors of the Grand Canal, seem to echo Proust's recollections of his wanderings through the city in *Albertine Gone*: "There it was easier to find those women of the common people, the matchmakers, the bead stringers, the glass and lace workers, the young factory workers in their great black shawls with fringes."

It is the granddaughter and great-granddaughter of Ettore Tito who welcome us into the palazzo where three generations of artists have lived and worked: Ettore Tito, the painter and sculptor whose precocious talents led his to being admitted to the academy at the age of twelve, his son the painter Luigi Tito, and his grandson the sculptor Pietro Giuseppe.

VENETIAN FASHION: JEWELRY

There have been goldsmiths in Venice since as early as 1233. From 1315, goldsmiths were granted the right to practice their craft within the strictly limited geographical parameters of the Rialto. The four most senior members of the guild, residents of Venice for at least twenty years, were allotted the onerous task of appraising the gold, silver, and finished works. The great ingenuity of Venetian goldsmiths was celebrated in a text by Leonardo Fioravanti in 1572. While they produced sacred objects on a substantial scale, their most famous creations were Manin gold chains or *intrigosa,* extremely fine chains fashioned from tiny rings of gold wire, using a technique that probably originated in Constantinople. Known as "Venetian chains," these became traditional pieces of jewelry handed down within families, often as dowries. Sadly, since the 1950s they have disappeared, owing to a shortage of craftsmen who still have the skills needed to make them.

As the gateway to the East, Venice quickly became an important trading hub for precious stones. Arab merchants would come to the city to sell diamonds, while travelers would bring back colored gemstones from their journeys. It was a seventeenth-century diamond-cutter from the Rialto, Vincenzo Peruzzi, who was credited with inventing a new way of faceting gemstones to enhance their brilliance. The "brilliant cut," with some fifty facets, is still used today.

The taste for jewelry among Venetian women, "coquettes and lovers of finery," was observed with a wry eye by George Sand: "The opulence of their toilette makes a curious contrast with the laxness of their habits." Since the nineteenth century, three famous Venetian names have perpetuated the arts of the goldsmith and jeweler: Missiaglia, Nardi, and Codognato.

FACING PAGE
In St. Mark's Square, the famous jeweler Nardi has specialized for three generations in the creation of exquisite Venetian jewelry. Giulio, the founder, Sergio, and now Alberto Nardi have reinterpreted familiar features of the Serenissima in jewelry, each with their favorite designs. Among the most iconic jewels of the house is the "Moretto," a small Moorish figure with a rich turban, first created in 1935 by Giulio Nardi.

BELOW
Jewelry and designs by Nardi. In 1960, fashionable themes for charm bracelets were inspired by Venetian symbols including the well, lion, and clock tower. Carlos de Beistegui was a great fan and gave them to his guests before his famous ball in 1951. Nowadays, Alberto Nardi concentrates on architectural motifs such as the Rialto Bridge and the Basilica of Santa Maria della Salute, while continuing the family heritage in the same premises as a century ago.

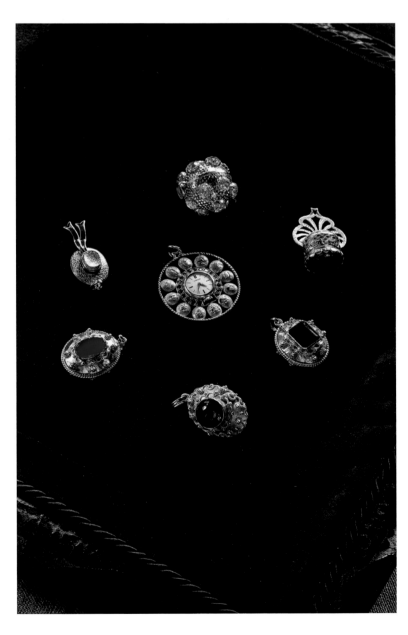

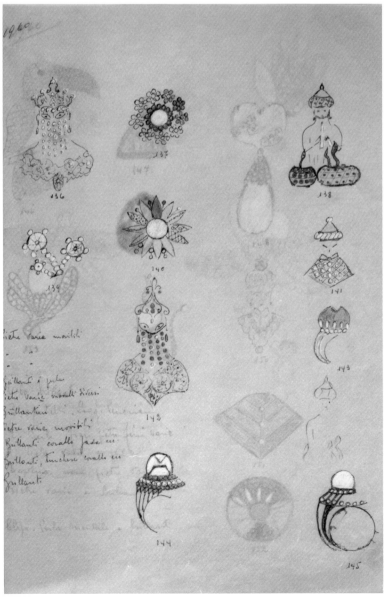

ABOVE AND FACING PAGE
The Codognato style: skulls
wearing crowns or set with
precious stones, the famous
memento moris, and
an entire eerie bestiary,
including the legendary
snake bracelet, reminiscent
of the decadent world of
Marchesa Casati.
RIGHT
Portrait of Attilio Codognato.

CODOGNATO

A veritable institution and an iconic destination for aesthetes,
"the quintessence of the Venetian soul" as Maurice Rheims wrote,
Codognato has occupied the same premises on the corner of Calle
Seconda dell'Ascensione and St. Mark's Square since the shop was
first opened in 1866 by Simeone Codognato. After first specializing in
paintings and antiques, the establishment soon also embraced the art
of jewelry. Fascinated by discoveries of Etruscan jewelry in Tuscany
and realizing how much interest these treasures would attract,
Simeone's son, Attilio Codognato, instigated a revolution in jewelry
and created an unmistakable style: a world of the vanitas, playing on
the macabre and the fantastical, and inspired by antiquity and
esoteric symbols. His jewelry was highly prized by the greatest artists
of the twentieth century, from Ernest Hemingway, Maria Callas, and
Sergei Diaghilev to Luchino Visconti, Jean Cocteau, and Andy Warhol.

Attilio Codognato, heir to this lineage of goldsmith-jewelers
and guardian of a unique savoir-faire, continues to mix Byzantine,
baroque, and neo-Gothic influences in jewelry that holds designers
and collectors in thrall—an essentially Venetian dramatic art.

DIAMANTI
FUMÉ

PIETRO

VENETIAN FASHION: SHOES

The mud and filth of the *calle* in sixteenth- and seventeenth-century Venice made it difficult to move around the city except by gondola. To raise their skirts above the muddy morass, Venetian women invented *zoccoli* or chopines, extravagantly lofty wooden clogs that could reach the dizzying height of sixteen inches (40 cm), and which remained in vogue until around 1660.

Cobblers and cordwainers, *calegheri* and *zapateri*, were present in Venice as early as the thirteenth century, had their own *scuola* on Campo San Tomà in San Polo from the fifteenth century, and took great pride in their patron saint, St. Aniano. It is not uncommon to find votive bas-relief shoe carvings on the sites where they used to have their shops. Every year, the guild of cordwainers would offer a symbolic gift of a pair of shoes to the Dogaressa. Today Venice is still famed for its shoes, even if the factories have moved to the nearby Brenta river.

"The Venetians attach far more importance to their shoes than to their clothes," observed the German poet and journalist August von Binzer in 1844. This passion is personified today by a unique designer-and-collector couple, Roberta and Luigino Rossi; the latter is the descendant of a family of shoe manufacturers who have been making models designed by the great couturiers since 1947. This couple have dedicated their lives to the art of the shoe, even setting up a shoe museum in the Villa Foscarini-Rossi in Stra, and have opened their home to us to reveal some of their personal collection of works of art inspired by footwear.

The most popular Venetian shoe today comes from the region of Friuli, from which it takes its name, the *friulane*. These light slippers were originally made from recycled materials such as old bicycle tires or scraps of fabric, sewn by hand. Initially adopted by gondoliers, who appreciated the way their softness and pliability protected the inside of their gondolas, they have gone on to become a resounding success throughout the world.

LEFT
A painting by Franco Gentilini hanging on one of Roberta Rossi's walls.

ABOVE AND FACING PAGE
Roberta Rossi, director of a design consultancy specializing in footwear, in her palazzo, where, with her husband Luigino, she has assembled an incredible collection of art dedicated to their favored theme.

PAGES 38–39
Luigino and Roberta Rossi's salon is a perfect illustration of Andy Warhol's "To shoe or not to shoe," with his shoe designs displayed on walls hung with Fortuny fabrics.

Views of the inner courtyard
of the Benedetto Marcello
Conservatory of Music.
Since 1876, the Conservatory
has been housed on
Campo San Stefano in the
monumental Palazzo Pisani,
the largest patrician palazzo
in the city, built in the
seventeenth century and
enlarged and remodeled
in the eighteenth century.
Its historical heritage
and library are among
the richest in Italy.

BELOW
President of the
conservatory, Giovanni Giol,
playing the piano in
the concert hall, formerly
the ballroom of the
Palazzo Pisani.

MUSIC IN VENICE

Venice is music. It was on Venetian territory that the luthier Ventura Linarol, who was to give the violin its definitive shape, was born in 1542. Other celebrated musicians born in Venice include Baldassare Galuppi, Claudio Monteverdi, Giovanni Gabrieli, Benedetto Marcello, Tomaso Albinoni, and, most famous of all, Antonio Vivaldi, the "red priest," who composed his *Four Seasons* in the city. Venice at that time had four "hospitals"—which were in fact musical conservatoires or *scuole*—and Vivaldi taught the orphan girls of the Hospedale della Pietà throughout his life. At once "a passion and an affair of state," according to Jean d'Ormesson, music reigned supreme in eighteenth-century Venice. Established in 1902 in the magnificent Palazzo Pisani, the Benedetto Marcello Conservatory of Music has taken the place of the *scuole* and continues to uphold values of excellence in music teaching in Venice.

The city was also the first to dedicate a performance space to opera, and to expand its audience beyond the nobility by allowing the public to attend. La Fenice Opera House, established in 1792, hosted the works of composers including Gioachino Rossini, Giuseppe Verdi, and Vincenzo Bellini, and its international reputation was to survive fires in 1836 and 1996.

In Venice music was also played in the open air, on boats and in squares. The orchestras in the cafés on St. Mark's Square are still there, but in the past the piazza was the setting for symphony concerts, staged several times every season and attended with religious devotion. During the Austrian occupation, military bands played the overtures to *Tannhäuser* and *Lohengrin* there, in Wagner's presence.

Venice was Richard Wagner's adopted city. "I want to remain here," he declared in 1858. His wish was realized: he died in Venice on February 13, 1883. Although his memory remains linked to his final home, Palazzo Vendramin Calergi, during the winter of 1858-59 Wagner lived and composed in another fifteenth-century Gothic residence, Palazzo Giustinian Brandolini d'Adda, on the Grand Canal.

WINNARETTA SINGER'S MUSICAL SOIRÉES

An outstanding figure on the Venetian musical scene in the early twentieth century, Winnaretta Singer, one of the heirs to the Singer Sewing Machine Company and wife of Prince Edmond de Polignac, acquired the Palazzo Contarini in 1901. She turned this dream residence on the Grand Canal, renamed the Palazzo Contarini-Polignac, into the venue for private concerts and some of the most sought-after musical evenings in Europe. An accomplished pianist herself, Winnaretta had a gift for spotting and fostering talent in others. A great patron of the arts, "Aunt Winnie," as she was affectionately known, supported artists such as Arthur Rubinstein and Vladimir Horowitz, and was tireless in commissioning new pieces from young musicians such as Gabriel Fauré and Claude Debussy. The long list of compositions created in her honor includes Stravinsky's *Renard*, Satie's

Socrate, and Fauré's *Cinq mélodies de Venise*, among many others.

Four of her pianos are preserved in the Palazzo Contarini-Polignac: an 1898 Pleyel, two Érards, one bearing her monogram, and a portable ship's piano made in London in 1896 by J.B. Cramer, with a five-octave keyboard on which Fauré and Reynaldo Hahn played, among others. In *L'Altana ou la vie vénitienne*, Henri de Régnier described an unforgettable serenade played by Hahn on a gondola on which the ship's piano had been installed.

Marie-Blanche de Polignac, Winnaretta's niece by marriage and only daughter of the fashion designer Jeanne Lanvin, was an excellent pianist and soprano who often came to the palazzo to play duets with her aunt. The Lanvin perfume Arpège was named in honor of her musical gifts.

PAGES 46-47
A grand piano stands
at the top of the staircase
leading to the piano nobile
of the Palazzo Falier.

ABOVE
Detail of the ceiling of the
piano nobile in the Palazzo
Giustinian Brandolini d'Adda,
where Richard Wagner
stayed during the winter
of 1858-59.

FACING PAGE
Portrait of Richard Wagner
by the engraver Rogelio
de Egusquiza, 1891.

PAGES 50-51
This unusual divan without
legs, the model for which
was in the Ca' Vendramin
when Wagner died there,
is preserved in the Palazzo
Polignac. Winnaretta Singer
was a fervent admirer
of the composer.

FACING PAGE
The reception room in the Palazzo Giustinian where Wagner installed his Érard piano, which he had brought from Zurich. Inspired by the song of a gondolier, he composed the shepherd's cantilena that opens the third act of *Tristan*. The walls are still lined with the red fabric he mentioned in his autobiography: "The grayish walls of my salon [...] did not go well with [...] a tasteful ceiling entirely painted al fresco. I therefore decided to have them covered with a very ordinary fabric, but in a dark red color."

RIGHT
An interior in the Palazzo Frigerio Zeno in Cannaregio. The palazzo is available for hire for concerts and evening events.

"Whenever I seek another word for 'music,' the only word I can find is 'Venice.'" **FRIEDRICH NIETZSCHE,** *Ecce Homo***, 1888.**

THE INDISPENSABLE GONDOLIER

Maneuvering his streamlined black gondola smoothly through the canals, wearing a straw boater trimmed with a ribbon and a red- or blue-striped top, the gondolier is perhaps the best-known symbol of Venice throughout the world.

The trademark striped top was a late introduction in the 1950s, when it was first worn by Alberto Sordi in the Dino Risi film *Venice, the Moon and You* in 1958. Tourists loved the outfit. It became legendary.

Not many people today are aware that gondoliers used to function in the domestic sphere. The grime and mud of the unpaved streets and the omnipresence of water meant that the city was impossible to negotiate on foot for Venetian ladies, to whom gondoliers provided an essential service. Unwaveringly loyal to the families who employed, fed, and frequently housed them, gondoliers *de casada* (of the house), would sport the colors and arms of the family they served.

They would have several liveries, the most elegant of which they would sport when guiding ceremonial gondolas, topped off with a curious tall hat known as the *baretta da gondolier* in place of the traditional straw boater.

In his Venice-set novel *Across the River and Into the Trees*, Ernest Hemingway, or rather, his literary avatar Colonel Cantwell, summed up the importance of the gondolier within the family and society, describing him as "unknowing, yet knowing all, solid, sound, respectful and trustworthy." When Marchesa Casati died in penury in London in 1957, her funeral was paid for by her personal gondolier.

The last gondolier *de casada* was employed by Contessa Annina Morosini; the last private gondolier worked for Peggy Guggenheim. Today, the profession has protected status and is limited to 433 gondoliers and 180 substitutes. It was opened up to women in 2010.

ABOVE
Late nineteenth-century photograph of a gentleman dressed as a gondolier (Arrivabene private archive). In her autobiography published in 1988, *Una gran bella vita*, Gabriella di Robilant gave an evocative description of the costume of her "two gondoliers, dressed in white, blue sashes round their waist, ribbons fluttering around their straw boaters, our silver coat of arms with Mocenigo roses on their arms."

FACING PAGE
Matteo Corvino's collection of miniature gondolas.

PAGE 56
Telegrams sent by the Zeno family to their gondolier in the early twentieth century shed a rare light on this relationship: "Cancel gondola today / weather dreadful will come tomorrow / vaporetto afternoon." The gondolier's buttons and epaulettes bear the Zeno coat of arms (Frigerio Zeno private archive).

PAGE 57
In the late nineteenth century whole families might pose in a gondola, even in the photographer's studio.

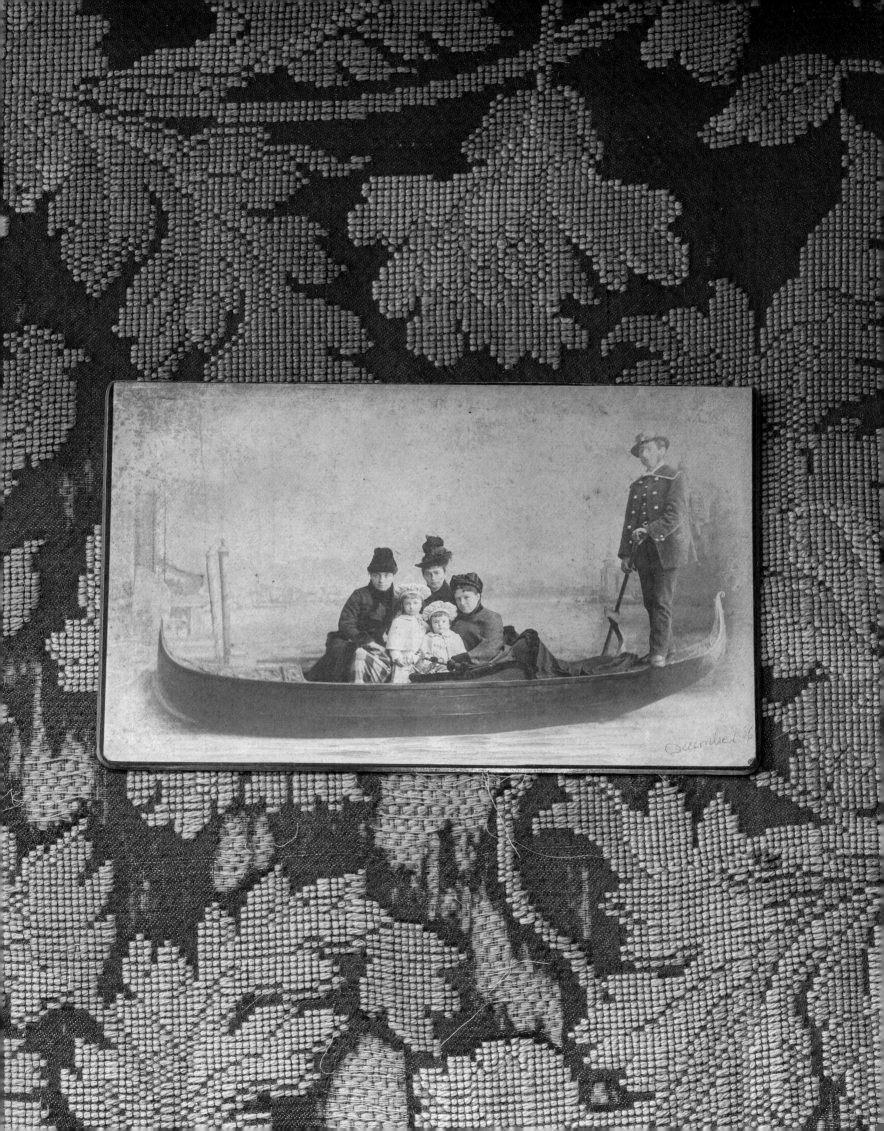

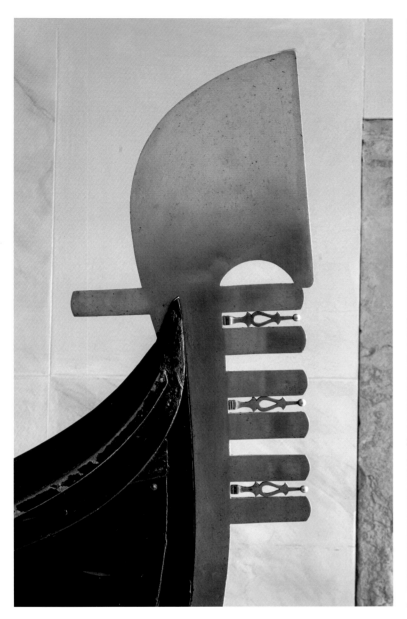

"It is always assumed that Venice is the ideal place for a honeymoon.
This is a grave error. To live in Venice or even to visit it means that you fall
in love with the city itself. There is nothing left over in your heart
for anyone else." **PEGGY GUGGENHEIM,** *Out of This Century*, 1979.

ABOVE LEFT
Detail of the *ferro* on
the bow of a historic gondola,
symbolizing the doge's cap
and the *sestieri*, the city's six
districts. The seventh tooth
on the opposite side signifies
the island of La Giudecca.

ABOVE RIGHT
In 1949, the American art
collector Peggy Guggenheim
bought the Palazzo Venier
dei Leoni on the Grand
Canal, which became
the headquarters of
the foundation and museum
bearing her name. Fascinated
by Venice, she lived there
until her death in 1979,
and was the last person to
employ a private gondolier.

FACING PAGE
A historic family gondola
still with its *felze*, the small
enclosed cabin that ensured
privacy and gave protection
from the weather. The long
black silhouette became
a legal requirement following
the passing of seventeenth-
century sumptuary laws to
prohibit ostentatious luxury.

ENTERTAINING, VENETIAN STYLE

GOURMET MEMORIES

Times have changed since the writer William Dean
Howells, American consul in Venice from 1861
to 1865, discovered with some dismay that "meat
and drink do not form the substance of conviviality
with Venetians ... that Venetian gayety is on few
occasions connected with repletion."

Princess Emanuela Notarbartolo di Sciara is the
author of *Il gioco della cucina* (The Kitchen Game).
Before her, her mother wrote a charming family
recipe book illustrated by Gio Ponti and Tomaso
Buzzi. When Servane Giol asked her to share some
of her precious Venetian recipes with her, Emanuela
gave a peal of laughter and exclaimed, "But Venetian
recipes are possibly the least amusing in the
whole of Italy!"

Cuisine in Venice focuses on fishing and hunting
in the lagoon. Vegetables—mainly artichokes
and petits pois—come from plots on the island of
Sant' Erasmo. And there is rice, lots of rice,
hence the Venetian way of inviting you to dinner:
Venga a mangiar quattro risi con me, meaning
"Come and eat four grains of rice with me."

This book would not be complete without
the recipe for the famous *Risi e bisi*, Risotto with
Petits Pois. Typically Venetian.

Menu

Consommé Vermicelle
Filets de Soles Frites Sauce Tartare
Noisette de Veau aux Petits
Poularde Sauce Américaine
Salade de Po
Asperges Sauce
Glace Vanille
Pâtis

LUNCH

CONSOMMÉ AILERONS
PAILLETTES AU CHESTER

SAUCE GRIBISH
MIGNONETTES DE VEAU RICHELIEU
CAILLES DE VIGNE PRINCESSE
SALADE MIRELLE
TITS SOUFFLÉS SIBÉRIENNE
AU DE MARIAGE
LES DE FRUITS

EZIA, IL 20 OTTOBRE 1924.

FACING PAGE
At home with Matteo
Corvino. On the wall lined
with Fortuny fabrics in
"narrow widths," which came
from another Venetian
palazzo, a painting by the
eighteenth-century French
artist Alexis Grimou depicts
a pilgrim on the way to
Santiago de Compostela.
On the sideboard sits the
Gelée à la Monet with pistou
and pistachio sauce.
RIGHT
Portrait of Matteo Corvino.

PAGE 66
A Franco-Italian dialogue in
the dining room, with a mirror
and gold-leaf table designed
by Matteo Corvino and 1940s
chairs by Marc du Plantier.
The Napoleon III table
centerpiece, inspired by the
Basin of Apollo at Versailles,
is complemented by a late
nineteenth-century Murano
bowl filled with antique
Venetian glass fruit, and
echoes the Roman bronze
horse recalling the Triumphal
Quadriga of St. Mark's
Basilica. Antique Saint-Louis
Thistle glasses, late
eighteenth-century famille
rose porcelain plates,
and Puiforcat cutlery on
placemats embroidered
with gold thread in Venice
and made for the Millennium
celebrations at Versailles
complete the setting.
PAGE 67
Detail of the Leopard
tapestry in the dining room.

RECIPE FOR *GELÉE À LA MONET*

Venetian designer of interiors and spectacular
events and parties, suggests this variation on
a recipe for tomato soup found in Claude Monet's
recipe notebooks: a Franco-Italian tribute to the
artist who, in 1908, at the age of sixty-eight, painted
the Serenissima tirelessly for two months, carried
away by the emotions the city aroused in him.
The room with a view and the small terrace where
he worked still exist in the St. Regis Hotel.

To serve 6
Take 2 cups / 450 ml good tomato purée
and add the same amount of vegetable
stock. Add a chopped onion, a bay leaf,
a spoonful of cane sugar and a small
bunch of basil and slowly bring to the boil.
Remove from the heat immediately
and strain while still warm.
Add salt and 4 tsp agar and pour
into a mold until set. Serve cold with
a pistou and pistachio sauce.

RECIPE FOR *RISI E BISI*

Ingredients for 6 servings
3 lbs. 4 oz. / 1.5 kg fresh petits pois in their pods
6 ¼ cups / 2 ½ pints / 1 ½ l stock
¾ stick of butter / 3 oz. / 80 g butter
1 medium-sized onion
1 lb. / 500 g Vialone Nano rice
2 slices / 60 g bacon
1 bunch parsley, finely chopped
½ cup / 4 fl. oz. / 125 ml white wine
¼ cup / 2 oz. / 50 g grated Parmesan cheese
Salt and pepper

Princess Emanuela Notarbartolo di Sciara explains:
"My father's name was Marco, like the patron saint
of Venice, and it is a family tradition that on his
feast day, April 25, which is also the city's feast day,
lunch begins with one of the most fragrant recipes
in Venetian cuisine, *Risi e bisi*, or Risotto with
Petits Pois. At that time of year, the best petits pois
in the world are to be found in the Rialto market.
According to tradition, each grain of rice should be
matched by a pea."

Pod the peas, wash the pods, and simmer them in
the stock over a low heat in a covered pan for at
least an hour. Then blend with an immersion blender
to give a liquid purée. Strain through a sieve to
remove any remaining fibers.

In another pan, melt half of the butter and sweat
the onion over a low heat until golden. Add the rice,
bacon, parsley, and petits pois, then gradually pour
the white wine in from a ladle. Pour in the peapod
stock, stirring constantly to stop the rice from
sticking. Cook for 18 minutes, taking care that
the rice does not dry out too much (Venetians say
the rice should be "on the wave"). At the end
of the cooking time, add the remaining butter
and the Parmesan cheese and season to taste.
Give the risotto a quick stir and serve hot.

ABOVE AND FACING PAGE
Servane Giol prepares
to serve the famous Risi
e bisi, the petits pois risotto
that is a great classic of
Venetian cuisine.

VENETIAN FESTIVALS AND CELEBRATIONS

PRIVATE EVENTS: THE DOGARESSA AND THE DOGALINA

Considered the most beautiful woman in Italy, Contessa Annina Morosini, the Dogaressa, dominated the Venetian party scene for over fifty years. This legendary beauty even conquered Kaiser Wilhelm II, and in 1885 she married the heir to one of the most illustrious families in Venice, Michele Morosini. They lived at the Ca' d'Oro and then at the Palazzo da Mula-Morosini in Dorsoduro. Left on her own in Venice after her husband moved to Paris, Annina began to hold a salon and to give dinners and balls, whether for her feast day, for that of the Redentore, for Carnival, or for the opening of the Fenice season.

Her invitations, written in green ink to match the color of her eyes, were eagerly anticipated. Her celebrated parties brought together crowned heads and the most distinguished names from the aristocracy and the artistic world. Her close friend the poet Gabriele D'Annunzio, who lived on the Grand Canal opposite the Palazzo da Mula, dubbed her "the fairy from the far side" or *Bellezza Vivente*—Living Beauty.

Implacably royalist in her beliefs, the Contessa displayed the Morosini coat of arms everywhere: on her palazzo, on her servants' liveries, on her carpets, gondolas, and plates—even on a diamond brooch. To reflect her narcissistic beauty, the palazzo was decorated throughout with mirrors and portraits of her. Instead of flowers, which she would toss into the Grand Canal from her balcony, she preferred gifts of precious metalwork—"something useful." Her last grand ball took place in 1946 in the presence of Umberto di Savoia, the last king of Italy. The end of Italian royalty marked the end of the receptions given by this prominent monarchist.

Another renowned hostess who left her mark on the art of Venetian entertaining in the last century was Gabriella di Giardinelli, the first wife of Andy di Robilant, who lived in the Palazzo Mocenigo from 1920 to 1932. Her autobiography, *Una gran bella vita* (A Great, Beautiful Life), paints a captivating picture of the social whirl of "balls, luxury, and privilege" that filled her years in Venice.

Dubbed La Bella Dogalina—a name she hated—by the poet Gabriele D'Annunzio, in tribute to the doges in her husband's lineage, Gabriella shook up life at the Palazzo Mocenigo. A close friend of Elsa Maxwell and Linda and Cole Porter, who was godfather to her second son, she gave her first costume ball on an eighteenth-century theme, removing costumes from their display cases in the Byron Room in the palazzo for the occasion. The highlight of the evening was the arrival of Elsa Maxwell casually sporting the ducal hat of Doge Mocenigo, which she had spirited away from his shrine. "The Morosini, Albrizzi, and Foscari ladies turned pale and the party was over. Following this episode, many Venetians were critical of our mania for inviting foreign guests."

The Diaghilev Ball, given in honor of Marina and Elizabeth of Greece, was one of Gabriella's most successful gala evenings, with Serge Lifar teaching each guest to perform a little choreographed entrance. More classical in style was one of her last balls, given in honor of the young Prince of Piedmont. Years later, Cole Porter would remember the servants in eighteenth-century livery, the immense red carpet at the palazzo entrance, the arrival of the gondola, and the tuberoses and pink irises, typical blooms of the lagoon, with their exquisite and haunting fragrance: "Venice was the most fantastic setting for balls, with the perfume of its flowers…"

Gala evenings at the Palazzo Mocenigo were to come to an end when Gabriella and her husband separated. The Dogalina left Venice to open a famous fashion house.

BELOW
With Contessa Papadopoli on the far left, guests at an eighteenth-century costume ball pose for photographer Giovanni Contarini (Arrivabene private archive).
FACING PAGE
Portraits of young Venetians in costume by Studio Vianelli, with one of Contessa Annina Morosini's coveted invitations to a soirée, written in green ink to match the color of her eyes (Frigerio Zeno private archive).

"Venice dresses for the ball.
Decked out with starry spangles,
Kaleidoscopic Carnival
Sparkles, teems and babbles."

THÉOPHILE GAUTIER, "Carnival," *Enamels and Cameos*, 1852.

FACING PAGE
A charming little gilt and patinated bronze bust of a child dressed as Harlequin by the Venetian sculptor Toni Luccarda (private collection). With its unmistakable multicolored lozenges, the costume of the commedia dell'arte hero was one of the most popular among the Venetians.

RIGHT
Contessa Frigerio Zeno's collection of antique fans, some decorated with Venetian tourist scenes, including views of gondolas and St. Mark's Square.

PAGE 76
Handwritten and illustrated menus from the Venetian Belle Époque frame a photograph of a ball in the Roaring Twenties (Frigerio Zeno private archive).

PAGE 77
Niki Arrivabene dressed in exotic costume, probably for one of the many balls given by Giuseppe Volpi (Arrivabene private archive).

Diner 31 Mars 1889.
Potage Printanière aux quenelles
Bouchées au foie gras et Attereaux à
l'Indienne
Bœuf à la mode au Madère
Côtelettes d'Agneau à la financière
Pâté de Faisans truffé
Asperges au beurre
Poulardes à la Périgord
Salade Parisienne
Gâteau St-Martin
Glace Ecume au Chocolat
DESSERT
Porto
Bordeaux, Château Lafite
Johanisberger - Champagne
Moscato di Setubal

11 Mars 1913
Potage Suzon
Canapés Windsor
Noix de veau à la Portugaise
Timballe Bontoux
Asperges sauce mousseline
Cailles farcies à la gelée - Salade
Parfait aux fraises
Castagnets blanc - Château Bages
Mumm - Muscatel Soleras

Roma 1883

Menu du 9 Juin 91
Consommé Célestine.
Langouste à la Parisienne
Quasi de veau truffé
à l'écarlate.
Asperges sauce Mousseline
Mousse de volaille
à la gelée.
Glace Alhambra
Dessert!

~ Diner du 15 Novembre 1909 ~
Potage Compiègne
Cabillaud Norvégien
Poularde en cocotte
Cebris au jus
Carré de veau - Salade
Glace Marie Louise
Dessert

Diner du 26 Juin 1903.
Consommé antagenic
Madéra secco 1847
Truite Breteuil sauce riche
Filet de bœuf à l'anglaise
Château Lafitte 1875
Soufflé de poulet Richelieu
Cailles truffées sur canapés
Champagne Mumm G.H.
Petits pois sucrés
Glace Alhambra
Baba au rhum
Madeira 1858
Dessert

Ballo mascherato
dell' 3 Settembre 1951
Palazzo Labia Venezia

Carta d'Ammissione che sara richiesta
all' entrata

694

Il Signor Carlos de Beistegui
ha l'onore d'invitare
Il Signor e la Signora Luccarda
a Palazzo Labia, Venezia
il 3 Settembre 1951
alle ore 22 h 1/2
R.S.V.P.

Ballo in costume del settecento Maschere e domino

PAGES 78–79
Carefully preserved in the family archives, Marjorie and Toni Luccarda's invitation to the masked ball given by Carlos de Beistegui in 1951 states baldly: "Ball in eighteenth-century costume. Masks and dominos." The album also includes photographs of the couple in their costumes, a beautiful odalisque for her, the painter Francesco Guardi for him. A Venetian sculptor who was "fascinated by the human face," Toni Luccarda immortalized the celebrities of Venetian high society, from Madina Visconti to Giovanni Volpi, via Ernest Hemingway. His silver or gilt bronze portrait busts preserve the memory of an "urbane and cosmopolitan Venice, seductive, with a hint of the Venice we love, of Venetian Venice" (Frédéric Vitoux).

ABOVE
A lace and mother-of-pearl fan: an indispensable accessory at balls in the past.

LEFT
The colored glass necklace and earrings worn by Marjorie Luccarda for Carlos de Beistegui's masked ball.

FACING PAGE
Marjorie Luccarda in her "oriental" costume, from the Paris couturier Tristan Maurice.

EXTRAORDINARY OCCASIONS:
THE VOLPI AND BEISTEGUI BALLS

Until the 1980s, the Volpi Ball was the most unmissable society event in Venice. One of the first of a long series of balls thrown by the influential Giuseppe Volpi took place in his Palazzo San Beneto on August 26, 1926, in honor of the Prince of Piedmont. A galaxy of famous painters and stage designers created the costumes on an oriental theme, including José Maria Sert for Contessa Nerina Volpi di Misurata and Umberto Brunelleschi for Maria Gaggia and the Marquess of Portago, not forgetting the Delphos gowns designed by Fortuny.

Under the magnificent ceiling painted by Ettore Tito, the guests opened festivities in the ballroom. Meanwhile the spectacle spread out on to the Grand Canal, where an enormous luminous pagoda floated amid hundreds of gondolas to the strains of Giuseppe Verdi.

Founders of the Venice Film Festival in 1932, Giuseppe Volpi and his family mixed the most celebrated actors with Venetian high society at their glittering balls.

In 1948, Don Carlos de Beistegui, heir to the vast fortunes of a prominent Spanish-American family, bought the Palazzo Labia. The building was in a lamentable state of repair, as a munitions ship had exploded nearby at the end of World War II, rocking it to its foundations. It would take three years to restore the baroque palazzo and its famous frescoes by Tiepolo.

The eighteenth-century-themed ball Beistegui threw on September 3, 1951 made him a "hero in a single night," according to Desmond Guinness. The "Ball of the Century," as it became known, is considered the "last of the great balls," even though the Volpis would continue to organize many more after this. The costumes sported by Jacques Fath, Baron de Redé, and Lady Diana Cooper have become the stuff of legend. How wonderful, then, to discover at Martina's home an intact treasure, the original costume worn by her mother, Marjorie, designed by her artist husband Tony Luccarda, and made in Paris by the couturier Tristan Maurice. The Luccardas—Marjorie dressed as a beautiful odalisque, Tony as the artist Francesco Guardi— were one of the few Venetian couples invited that evening.

The aura of the Beistegui Ball put Venice back on the map of the international jet set, just as Elsa Maxwell had earlier attracted high society back to the Lido. A trip to Venice was now de rigueur on the international social calendar and would remain so thanks to the Biennale.

ABOVE LEFT
The Basque-born Mexican billionaire Carlos de Beistegui, a great collector and aesthete, was the owner of the Palazzo Labia for just three years. The ball he gave on September 3, 1951 became legendary, however, as did his costume as the Procurator of Venice.
ABOVE RIGHT AND FACING PAGE
Inspired by the shows traditionally put on during Carnival, the "Human Pyramid" at Carlos de Beistegui's ball was sketched by Alexander Serebriakov, who left a famous series of watercolors of the high points of the evening.

POPULAR FESTIVITIES

Venice is a festival, an extraordinary experience every time, thanks to the magical alchemy of its palazzi, its gondolas, the reflections on its canals. Under the Republic, every political or religious ceremony was a pretext for processions, fireworks, popular fairs, or aristocratic balls, all culminating in Carnival, which went on for six months.

Venetian balls and festivals have evolved down the centuries. In the late nineteenth and twentieth centuries, the ball season was the month of September, with events vying with each other to dazzle not only the guests but also the crowds of Venetians who loved to watch the festivities from the Grand Canal, decorating their boats with multicolored lanterns to be part of the spectacle. Cole Porter, who lived through the Roaring Twenties in a vortex of endless parties, composed his most famous song, "Night and Day," in Venice. Following unforgettable parties at the Ca' Rezzonico, he would take the festivities out on to the water, renting a floating platform on which revelers would dance the Charleston to the strains of a jazz orchestra specially imported from Paris, between the yachts and the first battleships at the far end of St. Mark's Basin.

The most popular religious festivals are still the Festa del Redentore, on the third weekend of July, and the Festa della Madonna della Salute, on November 21. The faithful walk in procession to the two churches over temporary boat pontoons, in place for just a few nights. The Redentore festival features stunning fireworks displays let off from St. Mark's Basin, terraces, and quaysides, or—even more Venetian—from boats decorated with shells, lanterns, and flowers.

Political celebrations take the form of a historical regatta–the Regata Storica—on the first Sunday in September and the Vogalonga in May. The Vogalonga is something of a marathon for the gondoliers who compete for the title every year, but anyone can take part, from children to grandparents, as long as they can row eighteen and a half miles (thirty kilometers) across the lagoon. For the Regata Storica, ceremonial boats and gondolas and period costumes make quite a spectacle, along with the banners and tapestries displayed on the palazzo façades. The most sought-after parties are held in the palazzi that look out over the finish line, such as the Palazzo Inti Ligabue.

FACING PAGE
In a great Venetian tradition, crowds would throng the pavements along the canals and take to boats to watch the spectacles of festivals and regattas on the Grand Canal.

ABOVE
Guests arriving at Carlos de Beistegui's ball in 1951. Venetians crowded along the Grand Canal to watch the arrival of the thousand or so guests on four hundred gondolas.

THE DECORATIVE ARTS IN VENICE

VENETIAN CHINOISERIE

In 1298, when Marco Polo, the most famous of all Venetian merchants, wrote his *Book of the Marvels of the World*, afterwards known as *The Travels of Marco Polo,* on his return from his legendary travels across Asia, he gave one of the earliest descriptions of China through European eyes. In this book of traveler's tales, mingling factual information with sensory impressions, northern China, known as Cathay, was described as independent from the south, a division that would lead to lasting confusion over the Empire of Cathay and the Chinese Empire. It was this mythical land of Cathay, unmapped and inhabited by fantastical peoples and plants, that many historians believe to be the true inspiration for the vogue for chinoiserie.

A vision of China that was far removed from reality thus spread throughout Europe, based on travelers' tales and on rare objects decorated with scenes brought back by Spanish and Portuguese sailors in the sixteenth century. These flights of the imagination gave rise to chinoiserie, a fanciful vision of exoticism that ranged from simple imitation to the wildest interpretations, all in a strongly westernized taste. As a cultural phenomenon, this new decorative style was an immediate success, invading interior decoration and garden design and lasting for the next three centuries.

In Venice, this fascination with the Far East echoed the rococo style, which favored asymmetry, lightness, and an absence of chiaroscuro. Perhaps the most beautiful example of eighteenth-century chinoiserie is found in the anteroom wonderfully preserved in the Palazzo Papadopoli.

Oriental themes also took over stucco decorations and furniture, covering them with pagodas, gondolas, weeping willows, cherry trees, and exotic figures painted in gold on lacquer. Chinoiserie was designed to dazzle and amuse, and interior designs often mixed authentic Chinese objets d'art with their European interpretations.

From 1840 onwards, trade and military wars with China saw the dream of a fantasy Cathay vanish, but chinoiserie continued to adapt itself to European and American tastes. Throughout the twentieth century, influential decorators created unforgettable interiors on a chinoiserie theme, including Tony Duquette at the Palazzo Brandolini and Jacques Grange at the Palazzo Falier.

Chinese porcelain occupied a place of honor in Venetian interiors, which were populated with images of tropical inspiration influenced by orientalism, such as monkeys, shells, corals, and pearls. No palazzo was without its Foo dogs, dragons, and exotic plants and flowers. Magots or mandarins inspired costumes for Venetian balls, while boats transformed into Chinese junks paraded on the Grand Canal as public entertainments.

BELOW LEFT
The taste for chinoiserie lingered on in Venice, appearing as late as the twentieth century in designs by the jeweler Nardi.

BELOW RIGHT
Chinese-inspired costumes were a great success at costume balls, as in this photograph from around 1900 (Frigerio Zeno private archive).

FACING PAGE AND PAGES 90–91
Views of the chinoiserie antechamber in the Palazzo Papadopoli. Built in the mid-sixteenth century for the powerful Coccina family, then sold to the Tiepolo family in 1748, the palazzo was bought in 1864 by the Aldobrandini-Papadopoli brothers. The building was completely refurbished in 1875 under the direction of the Venetian interior designer and antiquarian Michelangelo Guggenheim.

FACING PAGE AND RIGHT
Details of the chinoiserie
antechamber in
the Palazzo Papadopoli.

A Chinese cabinet in
the small dining room
in the Palazzo Falier.
FACING PAGE AND PAGES 96–97
The large salon and office
on the piano nobile of
the Palazzo Falier. The interior
designer Jacques Grange
has transformed the piano
nobile, which had been
uninhabited for over one
hundred and fifty years, into
a warm and cheerful family
home. Retaining the beamed
ceilings and the raised loggia,
which is so well suited
to daily life, he combines
the refinement of Venetian
motifs—such as the silk
ceiling light by Venetia
Studium, a Fortuny design—
with orientalist notes such as
the pagoda chandelier.

LEFT
In the small dining room in the Palazzo Falier, lined with antique mirrors, Jacques Grange has chosen to strike an orientalist note.

FACING PAGE
Detail of a chinoiserie table with silver artichoke salt shaker and pepper grinder, indispensable accessories in any well-run Venetian household, made by the city's oldest goldsmith and jeweler, Missiaglia. Although the historic shop that opened in 1846 on St. Mark's Square is now sadly closed (though you can still make out its sign) the family's output continues to be a byword for excellence.

ABOVE AND FACING PAGE
An eighteenth-century
lacca povera bureau in the
Palazzo Polignac houses
a display of porcelain
figurines of magots and
mandarins.

FACING PAGE AND PAGE 105
A table setting on an
orientalist theme in Giorgio
Ceccato's dining room.
The Venetian Cozzi porcelain
service is inspired by Chinese
Imari motifs, the silver cutlery
with Meissen porcelain
handles is by the English
silversmiths Chawner & Co.
(1866), the A.VE.M glasses are
from an old Murano factory,
and the salt cellars are
Minotto hardstone.

ABOVE RIGHT
Portrait of Giorgio Ceccato.
PAGE 104
Some of the finest examples
of orientalism in Venice are
found in stucco decorations
of exceptional elegance,
as here in Giorgio Ceccato's
residence.

GIORGIO CECCATO

Giorgio Ceccato is the general secretary of Venetian Heritage,
a charity that works to preserve the city's heritage and restore
its works of art through cultural projects. His lives opposite the statue
of the famous Colleoni, commander-in-chief of the Serenissima's
armies in the fifteenth century, in a neighborhood that is still very
Venetian and lively. His windows open onto the magnificent Basilica
of San Giovanni e Paolo, dubbed the Venetian Pantheon because
of the number of doges who are buried there.

   Giorgio has a passion for tableware, especially blue-and-white
services with their playful, lighthearted version of orientalism. The
house already had some delightful oriental-style stucco decorations,
exact copies of those on the Villa Pisani, or La Barbariga, on the
Brenta, created by the famous Boccanegra, who collaborated with
Tomaso Buzzi. With the help of Federico Gorini, a Venetian antiques
dealer, Giorgio has hunted down an astonishing collection of
chinoiseries, magots, and other orientalist porcelain, adopting
the motto of the association's president, Peter Marino: "I don't want
to die rich, but surrounded by beautiful things."

THE MARK OF FAME: DAISY FELLOWES

Venice forges personalities, and their houses and palazzi reflect them. Every residence here is unique, and each one has a tale—or several—to tell. This is certainly true of the Palazzo Polignac, marked with the indelible stamp of Daisy Fellowes, one of the most elegant women of the twentieth century. The niece of Winnaretta Singer, Daisy married Prince Jean de Broglie, and after his death, Reginald Fellowes, a cousin of Winston Churchill. She spent a great deal of time at her Aunt Winnaretta's Palazzo Polignac, redecorating the charming library salon in her own assured and elegant taste, or covering the walls of a bathroom with stucco daisies in a visual *fantaisie* inspired by her name.

A photograph in the small salon at the Palazzo Polignac shows her in all the splendor of the costume she wore to Carlos de Beistegui's ball in 1951. Regularly voted the world's best-dressed woman by fashion magazines in France and America, Daisy Fellowes won first prize that evening for her tableau vivant of the Queen of Africa, inspired by Tiepolo's *Allegory of the Planets and Continents* at the Würzburg Residenz in Bavaria. Immortalized by Cecil Beaton, she poses in front of the great fresco in the Palazzo Labia in a sublime white silk and taffeta dress trimmed with leopard print, specially created by Dior, accessorized with the iconic Tutti Frutti Indian-style necklace by Cartier.

ABOVE
Daisy Fellowes wearing Schiaparelli with the Indian-inspired Tutti Frutti necklace by Cartier, portrait by Cecil Beaton, 1936.
FACING PAGE
Displayed on a gueridon in the small salon at the Palazzo Polignac are two photographs of Daisy Fellowes, one of them the portrait taken by Cecil Beaton at the Beistegui Ball in 1951.

BELOW AND FACING PAGE
Daisy Fellowes' bathroom
at the Palazzo Polignac.
The stucco daisy decoration
recalls a similar motif on
the walls of a room
in the Palazzo Grimani.

THE MARK OF FAME:
MARIANO FORTUNY

Mariano Fortuny was born in Granada in 1871, son of the then-famous Spanish painter Mariano Fortuny y Marsal, but it was in Venice that this multifaceted genius was to give full expression to his talents. In 1898, he transformed the large fifteenth-century Gothic Palazzo Pesaro degli Orfei, on Campo San Beneto, into a house-studio. This was the workshop where printed velvets and silks were woven—printed cottons were produced in the Giudecca factory (see p. 197)—as well as being the laboratory for his multiple gifts as engraver, sculptor, painter, photographer, set designer, and decorator. "I have been interested in many things, but my true métier remains that of a painter," he admitted, and in parallel with all his other activities he exhibited his paintings at the Biennale from 1924 to 1942. Fortuny's studio was gifted to the city of Venice in 1956 by his wife and muse, Henriette, and has since been turned into a museum that has just opened again after a restoration campaign lasting several years. The design by Pier Luigi Pizzi plunges the visitor into the heart of a singular and singularly Venetian universe.

FACING PAGE AND ABOVE LEFT
In his studio in the Palazzo Pesaro degli Orfei, now the Museo Fortuny, the artist worked from 1910 until the end of his life on this trompe l'oeil decoration of a winter garden, a huge tempera composition mounted on a stretcher. The layout of the room is as designed by Fortuny.
ABOVE RIGHT
Mariano Fortuny, photographed around 1900.

THE MARK OF FAME:
RENZO MONGIARDINO

As the creator of some of the most theatrical interiors of the twentieth century, Renzo Mongiardino undoubtedly drew inspiration for his work from his experience and training as a theater and film set designer. He did not define himself as an interior designer, but rather as a creator of atmospheres who liked to play with appearances. "He was more interested in faux marble than in the real thing, and for him trompe-l'oeil was as much a moral code as an aesthetic," wrote Frédéric Vitoux in *L'Art de vivre à Venise*. "While it is true that Mongiardino was not Venetian—he was born in Genoa in 1916—to feel such a love for the elegance of the show, of performance, is to be a Venetian at heart." Possessed by a painter's vision, this master of illusion mingled colors and motifs, sumptuous

fabrics, and trompe-l'oeil in way that was unique to him. In dining rooms, for example, he loved to position two round tables to theatrical effect.

Cristina Brandolini discovered him when he was still unknown, and together they embarked upon a redesign of the interiors of the Palazzo Giustinian-Brandolini, still inhabited by three generations of the same family. Aided by the painter Lila de Nobili, Mongiardino conceived brilliantly inventive and unexpected solutions there, as in this small, low-ceilinged room on the top floor, now the studio of the artist Marcantonio Brandolini d'Adda. Here, Mongiardino created fragments of an imaginary chapel, an illusory mosaic of faux cracks in the walls, faux veils topped by the bust of a saintly bishop, gazing heavenwards to create a faux perspective. An ideal aerie for an artist.

ABOVE AND PAGES 114–15
On the top floor of the Palazzo Giustinian-Brandolini, Mongiardino designed an impressive decorative scheme creating the illusion of a chapel by means of a dramatic layout and trompe-l'oeil frescoes of architectural features. It is now the studio of the artist Marcantonio Brandolini d'Adda.

FACING PAGE
On the dining room table are models of glass pieces designed by the artist's mother, Marie Brandolini, founder of Laguna~B.

"When I went to Venice, I discovered that my dream had become—incredibly, but quite simply—my address." **MARCEL PROUST, letter to Madame Émile Straus, April 24, 1910.**

FACING PAGE AND PAGES 118–19
In 1980, Victoria Press bought a beautiful piano nobile on the Grand Canal. In it she discovered two eighteenth-century allegorical grisailles, dessus-de-portes that she decided to complement with her friend Darko Petrovic, a set designer for theater, opera, and ballet. Together they had fun creating pastiches of the original paintings and slipping in visual jokes, rather like Tiepolo in his time, with the twenty-first century suddenly erupting into view in the form of a wheelie suitcase or a cell phone.

SYMBOLS OF VENICE: THE LION

The lion is the symbol of Mark the Evangelist in the tetramorph, the depiction of the four winged animals pulling the chariot in the vision of the Old Testament prophet Ezekiel. Already adopted as personifications of the four cardinal points in Babylonian culture, these creatures now became associated with allegories of the four evangelists: the lion for Mark, the bull for Luke, the eagle for John, and the human figure for Matthew.

St. Mark was adopted as patron saint of the city of Venice in 828, succeeding the Graeco-Byzantine warrior St. Theodore. Statues of the two saints dominate the entrance to St. Mark's Square. The choice of the evangelist as protector of Venice is attributed to a vision in which an angel appeared to Mark, promising him rest in this spot. The saint's relics, stolen from Alexandria by Rustico da Torcello and Bon da Malamocco on the orders of the Doge Giustiniano Partecipazio, were brought back to Venice in a picaresque venture. The basilica was then rebuilt to provide a suitably holy resting place.

In 1260, the winged lion became the symbol of the Venetian Republic. Often depicted with a halo to emphasize its sacred associations and accompanied by a book—open to symbolize peace, closed to symbolize war—it is still the city's emblem. The flag of the Republic of Venice featured the lion with the six districts of the city, the *sestieri*. Every year, the highest prize awarded at the Venice Film Festival is the Golden Lion.

The lion may be depicted in three different positions, *andante*, *rampante*, or *moleca*. *Andante* shows it walking in profile, supported on three legs and with the fourth leaning on an open book. *Rampante* is for times of war, with a closed book and a brandished sword. *Moleca* shows the lion frontally, seated and with wings spread, looking like a crab with its claws open (the meaning of *moleca* in the Venetian dialect). This version was frequently used to fit into restricted spaces such as coins and bas-reliefs.

FACING PAGE
The magnificent façade of the Scuola Grande di San Marco, richly decorated with colored marble, bas-reliefs, and statues, including the winged lion of St. Mark, symbol of the Republic of Venice.
ABOVE
One of the two lions framing the entrance to the Scuola Grande di San Marco, a marble bas-relief by Tullio Lombardo.

BELOW AND FACING PAGE
In Gigi Bon's studio
(see p. 272), the *rampante*
lion appears as a cut-out
decoration and on a banner.

"[A]nd a dying Glory smiles
O'er the far times, when many a subject land
Looked to the winged Lion's marble piles,
Where Venice sate in state, throned on her hundred isles!"

LORD BYRON, *The Pilgrimage of Childe Harold,* 1812–18.

"Although one had seen all the cities of the world, there would still be a surprise in store for him in Venice. The sight of a town whose towers and mosques rise out of the water, and of an innumerable throng of people where one would expect to find only fish, will always excite astonishment."

MONTESQUIEU, *Persian Letters*, 1721.

FACING PAGE
On Cathy Vedovi's walls, the marine theme takes the form of mermaid sconces by Georges Jouve, found in the Pierre Passebon gallery.

ABOVE
Mosaic with fish, from a bathroom in the Palazzo Falier. Although the fish is not strictly speaking a symbol of Venice—even if the shape of the city when seen from above is strangely reminiscent of one—it nevertheless occupies an important place in this city on a lagoon, where aquatic motifs and creatures including fish, crustaceans, and mermaids often appear both in the external and internal decorations of the palazzi.

LEFT AND FACING PAGE
Cathy Vedovi, a French-Canadian interior designer and major collector of contemporary art, made this Venetian palazzo her own in early 2020. All her interiors are inspired by one or more works of art. In the dining room with its rattan furniture found in Italy and France, it was a fish-shaped fireplace by the sculptor François Melin. On the table, a tablecloth inspired by Burano fishing nets, fish dishes and plates in Vallauris pottery, glasses by Giordana Naccari, and spoon candelabra by the sculptor Arman.

MONOPOLIES ON THE EXTRAORDINARY

MIRRORS

INVENTED BY THE VENETIANS,
RIVALED BY THE FRENCH

Mirror, glimmer, shimmer... words that might have been invented to describe the canals and the light of the Serenissima. Only Venice, city of myriad reflections, could have inspired the fabulous creation of the mirror. The Italian language has a word, moreover, to describe the play of light on water and the flickering reflections on the palazzo walls: *gibigiana*. Hard to translate, it denotes the flashes, gleams, and scintillations of light on a reflective surface, such as glass, or the water in the canals. The invention of the mirror was a response to this quest for perfection in reflection.

Documented since the first century CE, the manufacture of mirror glass was given fresh impetus from 1440, when a Venetian, Angelo Barovier, invented crystal or transparent glass, which proved a huge step forward in the manufacture of spectacle lenses. A century later, Vincenzo Rador of Murano patented the technique of making mirrors by combined this transparent, smooth-surfaced glass with a reflective surface, the composition of which varied over time.

Mercury mirror glass made its first appearance in Venice in the fifteenth century. At the time, this was the only manufacturing technique that could achieve such high reflectivity and purity. Made from a cylinder of blown glass split and flattened on a stone, these mirrors could only be very small in size. Costly and damaging to health, the process of making the mercury-tin amalgam used in this type of mirror, which claimed the lives of so many young apprentices, was eventually banned. In 1835, a German chemist, Justus von Liebig, discovered a method for coating the surface of the glass with a fine layer of aluminum or silver, a technique still in use today.

So great was the renown of Venetian mirrors during the Renaissance that the Republic introduced a draconian system of checks and controls to protect its monopoly. Mirror makers were forbidden from leaving the island of Murano or speaking to foreigners, while revealing the secrets of the manufacturing process was made punishable by death, with severe repercussions for members of the traitor's family. For those who protected the monopoly, conversely, rewards, privileges, and marriage alliances with the nobility were promised.

One of the most fervent admirers of Venetian mirrors was the French king Louis XIV, who launched a vogue for them in France between 1665 and 1670. Imports of Venetian mirrors increased massively to satisfy an ever-growing demand, and this passion proved so expensive—costing some 100,000 ecus annually (approximately 3.25 million dollars today)—that it prompted Colbert, Comptroller-General of Finances, to set up a glass manufacturer on French soil without delay. As early as 1665, he sent a secret agent to go and live in Murano and set up an escape route to Paris for its glassmakers, so initiating the first known case of industrial espionage in Europe. A number of wildly improbable undercover operations involving the poaching of Venetian glassworkers were hatched until 1667.

In this "war of mirrors," the Republic resorted to threats and poisoning, followed by promises of absolution for those who chose to return to the fold. Three celebrated glass masters, Barbini, La Rivetta, and Crivano, returned to Venice. In France, the Manufacture Royale des Glaces à Miroirs was founded in 1665, and from that point on Colbert imposed a veto on the import of Venetian products.

PAGE 128
Detail of the engraved mirrors in Bar Longhi at the Gritti Palace.
PAGE 129
Detail of the hall of mirrors in the Palazzo Falier.
FACING PAGE
An antique mirror with floral decoration painted by Mariano Fortuny's father (Venice, Museo Fortuny). The imposing carved and gilded wooden frame is embellished with foliage and a trio of busts of cherubs.

HALLS OF MIRRORS

In the eighteenth century, mirrors became an outward sign of wealth for the most powerful families. Mirrors of large dimensions were more valuable than the paintings of famous artists, and some were encased in sumptuous frames. As the size of mirrors increased, so entire rooms in baroque palaces were lined with them. The vogue for these mirrored rooms, or *Spiegelkabinett*, spread throughout Europe, especially in northern countries. Venice also boasted its mirrored spaces, the most celebrated of which are probably the salons of the famous Caffè Florian on St. Mark's Square, the fashionable hub of Venetian social life and a favorite haunt of distinguished figures.

Few of Venice's private palazzi still possess rooms lined with mirrors. Two rare examples are revealed here, the first in a palazzo overlooking the Grand Canal, the second in a residence in Dorsoduro. Of different periods and origins, they illustrate perfectly the infatuation of previous centuries for these remarkable interiors.

FACING PAGE, ABOVE, AND PAGES 134–35
The Palazzo Falier boasts a rare example of a Venetian hall of mirrors, with characteristic painted boiseries and play of mirrors multiplying the space and light.

FACING PAGE AND RIGHT
The delicacy of a Royal
Copenhagen Flora Danica
porcelain tea service
echoes the refinement
of the antique mirrors
lining the walls.

"The bar was just across from the lobby of the Gritti....
The colonel looked out of the windows and the door of the bar onto the
waters of the Grand Canal. He could see the big black hitching post for
the gondolas and the late afternoon winter light on the wind-swept water....
'Two very dry Martinis,' the Colonel said. 'Montgomerys. Fifteen to one.'"

ERNEST HEMINGWAY, *Across the River and into the Trees*, 1950.

ABOVE AND FACING PAGE
Bar Longhi at the Gritti
Palace, famed for its
engraved mirrors. The vogue
for mirrors incised or painted
to create reflections or
decorative effects originated
in the seventeenth century.
The Gritti Palace is also
famed for its guests,
including Ernest Hemingway,
who stayed there several
times between 1948
and 1954.

"The timeworn mirror like water, shimmering and moist."

HENRI DE RÉGNIER, "Le Pavillon," *La Cité des Eaux*, 1902.

ABOVE AND FACING PAGE
Transposed to Venice from
Rome, the hall of mirrors
in the Casa Cicogna in
Dorsoduro has a dramatic
draped ceiling with a modern
Fortuny chandelier.

VENICE: A PRIVATE INVITATION

140

"Venice is a mirror, art is its reflection."

FRANÇOIS DE BERNARD, *Le miroir de Venise*, 2021.

ALESSANDRO DIAZ DE SANTILLANA

Descended from the Venini, one of the most illustrious dynasties
of Murano glassmakers of which his grandfather Paolo was a founder,
Alessandro Diaz de Santillana was almost literally born into a glass
factory. He recalls a decisive turning point in 1999, when, while he was
admiring the hanging mirrors in the Palazzo Polignac, he had a vision
that would determine his life's work, a flash of understanding of
the alchemy by which glass is transformed into a mirror.

His childhood fascination with old mercury mirrors, damaged and
worn by time, led him to start researching into the colors of metal
oxidation. He developed and perfected the ancient technique of
"blind" mirrors: mirrors that make all reflections impossible through
processes such as destructuring, opacity, inversion, and shattering.
A "sculptor in glass and anti-mirrors," Alessandro Diaz de Santillana
finds his inspiration in water and the non-reflections of pools
and puddles.

RIGHT
Alessandro Diaz de
Santillana, *Untitled*, 2017,
Palazzo Falier. Positioned
behind a Murano crystal
chandelier, the wall
installation consists
of two large interlocking
cloisonné discs that split
and refract the light.

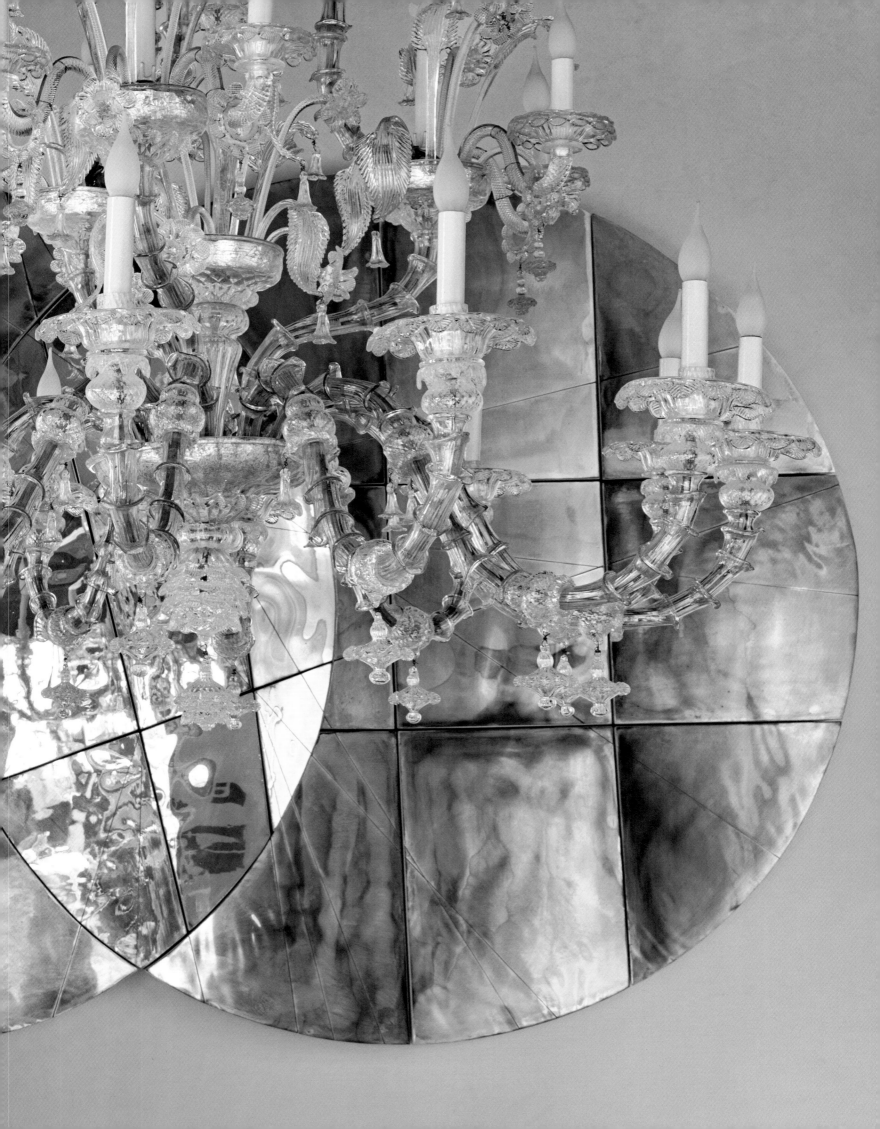

LEFT
Trapezoid was specially
commissioned from
Alessandro Diaz de Santillana
by Matteo Corvino to echo
a fragment by the painter
Filippo De Pisis, found in
a garbage dump by his dog
and now displayed opposite.

FACING PAGE
Suspended from the ceiling
in this private palazzo is
Gondola by Alessandro Diaz
de Santillana (private
collection).

PAGES 148–49
In a salon in Matteo Corvino's
palazzo, a large pier glass
between the windows opens
up the space and intensifies
the light.

"Who sees the human face correctly:
the photographer, the mirror, or the painter?"

PABLO PICASSO, in Isabelle de Maison Rouge, *Picasso*, 2016.

BELOW AND FACING PAGE
In the Palazzo Loredan
dell'Ambasciatore, a rare and
exceptional mirror from the
first half of the eighteenth
century: composed of small
fragments of mirror glass,
it creates a palazzo façade
that looks like a reflection.

S.A.L.I.R.

Founded in 1923 by Giuseppe d'Alpaos, Decio Toso, and Guglielmo Barbini, Studio Ars Labor Industrie Riunite has produced some of the finest mirrors and decorations on glass in Venice in recent decades. Renowned for its traditional mirror production processes, specializing in engraving using an engraving wheel, and sandblasting, and a master in the use of gold and enamel, the Murano-based company employed engravers, sandblasters, and specialists in eighteenth-century imitations. In the past, enamel work was reserved for women and mirror work for men, and this division was reflected in the distribution of the work space, with women working downstairs and men upstairs.

The finest artists have collaborated with S.A.L.I.R., such as the painter Vittorio Zecchin, who created the magnificent workshop doors, Gio Ponti, Piero Fornasetti, and Ettore Sottsass. Their work has been exhibited and won prizes throughout Italy and Europe.

ABOVE
Specialists in the manufacture of traditional Venetian mirrors, S.A.L.I.R. had over a thousand different models in its catalogue.

FACING PAGE
The process of making a mirror would begin with the choice of the frame, cut using one of the wooden templates in the workshop and made by skilled carpenters.

GLASS

MURANO GLASS: A PEERLESS CREATION

Born of sand and fire, glass is one of the oldest materials used by humans, making its first appearance in Mesopotamia and Egypt in the second millennium BCE. The earliest known manufacturing formula appears on the clay tablets of the Assyrian king Ashurbanipal, dating from the seventh century BCE and specifying "60 parts sand grains, 180 parts seaweed ash, 5 parts chalk." In the Middle Ages, it was in Venice that the method of producing the most transparent and delicate glass ever created was developed. The city's geographical location and its abundance of raw materials—silica extracted from sand and soda obtained from the combustion of seaweed from the East—combined with the presence of Byzantine artists exiled after the fall of Constantinople, played an important part in the rise of glassmaking.

As early as 1291, the glass furnaces were transferred from Venice to the island of Murano in order to prevent fires, and above all to enable the Republic to protect the secrets of the glass manufacturing process more effectively. From 1441, foreigners were forbidden from owning furnaces and glassmakers from leaving Venetian territory. A whole system of rewards and reprisals was devised to keep the monopoly exclusive. The entire history of Murano is littered with rivalries and intrigues.

Even today, its secrets are jealously guarded and handed down from one generation to the next.

The art of glassmaking reached its peak in Venice between the fifteenth and seventeenth centuries. It retained its unrivaled status thanks to the expertise of the master glassmakers and the cultural climate of the Italian Renaissance, of which it became one of the most coveted treasures. The Venetian monopoly on glass manufacture, the *Bulla communis Venetiarum*, provided the city with one of its most important economic revenues. Venetian glassmakers were masters of the arts of transparency, color, and a rich palette of decorations. They experimented with and developed numerous techniques, including milky-white opaque *lattimo* glass, aventurine obtained by adding copper crystals, filigree, and millefiori. Glass beads, meanwhile, were produced exclusively in Murano from the fifteenth to eighteenth century.

These prestigious and enduring inventions were to enable Murano glass to maintain its excellence for many years after it had lost its monopoly. Murano glass companies can also boast of exceptional longevity, with Barovier and Toso in business since 1295. Barovier, whose forebear invented crystal in 1440, is believed to be one of the oldest firms in the world.

"As a Venetian glass knows
in coming into being this gray
and the wavering light
with which it will be smitten."

RAINER MARIA RILKE, "Comme un verre de Venise," *Vergers*, 1924–25.

"At the end of the blow pipes the molten glass swelled, twisted, became silvery as a little cloud, shone like the moon, cracked, divided into a thousand infinitesimal fragments, glittering and thin ... the half-formed cup was again exposed to the heat, then drawn from it docile, ductile, sensitive to the lightest touches that ornamented and refined it, conforming it to the model handed down by their ancestors, or to the free invention of a new creator."

GABRIELE D'ANNUNZIO, *The Flame*, 1900.

FACING PAGE
A stunning 1960s glass
chandelier dominates this
kitchen at the Palazzo
Bernardo.

FACING PAGE AND RIGHT
The ceiling of the mirrored
bar by Seguso in this private
palazzo is inspired by
the one of the Al Todaro bar
in St. Mark's Square, where
the owner used to enjoy
ice creams as a child.

THE CHANDELIER:
A TECHNICAL TOUR DE FORCE

To compete with the Bohemian crystal chandeliers that were in vogue in Europe in the early eighteenth century, another Venetian, Joseph Briati, invented the method known as *chiocche*, literally meaning "strands," which is still in use today. Thanks to this method, using a metal structure sheathed in tubes of glass and covered with flowers, leaves, and fruit in blown glass, the multiarmed chandelier was born. Whether in monochrome or colored glass, it was characteristically Venetian. The structure made it possible to push the earlier limitations on size and volume further than ever before, since the arms of the chandelier could now be of any length. Thus the *barchetta* chandelier, among others, came into being, with an elongated oval shape reminiscent of a small boat or gondola.

After the virtuoso technical advances of the eighteenth century, in the nineteenth century the Venetian glass industry experienced a marked slow-down. The Habsburg monarchy favored Bohemian crystal, and imposed limits and heavy taxes on the import of raw materials to Murano. It was to be the creative community—artists, designers, and architects—who would breathe new life into Venetian glass in the twentieth century.

With the inauguration of the first Biennale in 1895, and later the Venezia Pavilion dedicated to the decorative arts, major names in the art world collaborated with master glassmakers to create outstanding pieces. The Venini, Seguso, and Barovier families from Murano now embarked increasingly on collaborations with Italian designers, followed by international creators. Today, unique pieces by Ettore Sottsass, Gio Ponti, Vittorio Zecchin, Carlo Scarpa, and Napoleone Martinuzzi, among others, are highly sought after by collectors.

ABOVE
A 1950s sconce by Seguso (Alessandro Zoppi collection), inspired by the *fano*, the three-light lantern formerly displayed on the stern of Venetian ships.

FACING PAGE
A Venetian dining room dominated by a breathtaking Murano glass chandelier.

LEFT
An eighteenth-century
barchetta chandelier
in the Palazzo Loredan
dell'Ambasciatore. With its
interplay of transparent and
opaque glass, the way it
captures and refracts light,
and the imaginative flair
of its colors and shapes, it
showcases all the excellence
of the Venetian glass
masters.
FACING PAGE
Giorgio Ceccato's salon,
looking out over the Basilica
of Santi Giovanni e Paolo
and the Scuola Grande
di San Marco, is embellished
with a beautifully colored
chandelier.

MARCANTONIO BRANDOLINI D'ADDA

Born in Venice, Marcantonio Brandolini d'Adda lives and works in
the city as an artist and designer, with the art of glassmaking lying
at the heart of his training. His mother Marie Brandolini founded
the Laguna~B company in 1994, creating contemporary versions
of the classic Venetian wine glass, or *goto*. In his unique sculptures,
Marcantonio Brandolini d'Adda explores the techniques of blown
glass and the formal possibilities of abstract compositions in which
he reinterprets the tradition of *cotissi*. He applies these fragments
of glass and leftovers from firings to monochromatic blocks of pure
glass to create rugged forms resembling rocky landscapes.
His works, including his *Vessels* series, are exhibited in Europe from
London to Milan, and during Glass Week, the showcase for Venetian
glass held every September. Marcantonio Brandolini d'Adda brings
new perspectives to works in glass in contemporary art, while
at the same time responding to the major challenges of ecological
sustainability now facing Murano.

RIGHT AND PAGES 176–77
While the passion of Pierre Rosenberg, former president and director of the Louvre, for seventeenth- and eighteenth-century paintings and drawings is well known, his collection of glass animals is more unexpected. The interest was born by chance in a Venetian restaurant: "I have been collecting since I was a child, stamps, marbles; the idea of accumulating has always been a part of me. The passion for glass came later, some thirty years ago, when I started spending time in Venice." A great collector, this famous French academician describes himself as insatiable, and the seven hundred and fifty pieces displayed at the Stanze del Vetro in 2021 were only a small part of the playful and highly decorative collection that has taken over his Venetian palazzo.

CHAHAN MINASSIAN AND RICHARD MAKIN-POOLE

A mixture of East and West, of gold and mirrors, Venice, a city between two worlds, has gradually become more and more compelling to Chahan Minassian, a Lebanese of Armenian origin whose work has always reflected this opulence, this fusion of cultures. For him, it is "the coexistence of all beauties, a showcase of nomadic inspiration, a jewel."

A renowned interior designer, gallerist, designer, and collector, Chahan is one of those who, like Zecchin before him, understands the essence of glass. As producer and collector, Chahan revisits Venetian excellence, from glass to mirrors, from fabrics to table linen, from bronze to jewelry. Thus, a new collection inspired by Venice is born: chandeliers, lamps, photophores, and a coffee table with the evocative name of "Canal Grande," fine stripes in "Chahanian" colors, shades of green and pink. His personal collection is dominated by the great names in the art of glassmaking from the 1920s to the 1950s: Napoleone Martinuzzi and his cacti, Barovier, Barbini, Gio Ponti, Carlo Scarpa, and Ettore Sottsass. The palazzo in which he lives with his partner, Richard Makin-Poole, is a cabinet of curiosities that reflects an artistic journey consisting of encounters like the one with the Santillana siblings, Laura and Alessandro. The apotheosis of the art of fusion.

FACING PAGE

In the alcove, a collection of glass from 1920 to 1950, by Martinuzzi, Barbini, and Barovier, in an iridescent palette of gold, taupe, pink, and green. "The master glassmakers, particularly those of the early twentieth century, have inspired and fascinated me in the sobriety of their forms, the mastery and perfection of the symmetries of their objets, while also bringing different textures and transparencies to every piece," says Chahan Minassian. On the wall is an important collection of ceramics from Ancil Farrell's brutalist series.

ABOVE RIGHT

With his partner Richard Makin-Poole and their two French bulldogs, Oscar and Violet, Chahan Minassian chose Venice for the sophistication and ease of its way of life, at once contemporary and traditional.

PAGE 180

A joyous assortment of antiques and bespoke items: the water glasses are from Giordana Naccari at L'Angolo del Passato, and the wine and champagne glasses were designed by Chahan, as were the bubble-glass plates. The candlesticks are by Pauly.

PAGE 181

Chahan Minassian: "I am a collector who likes to share and entertain." On Chahan's wrist is a rare Nardi charm given by Carlos de Beistegui to his guests.

RIGHT
On the Queen Anne table
by Paul Evans (1969), with
matching chairs upholstered
in Bevilacqua Tortue velvet
and fine milleraies suede
by Chahan Minassian, stands
a rare red and gold ensemble
of two columns and a
mermaid by Alfredo Barbini
for Napoleone Martinuzzi
(1958), with a mobile
sculpture by James Turnbull.

FACING PAGE

Alessandro and Alessandra Zoppi possess one of the finest collections of Venetian glass from the eighteenth to the twentieth centuries, grouped by form and color, as on this dresser.

ABOVE RIGHT

Portrait of Alessandra Zoppi.

ALESSANDRO AND ALESSANDRA ZOPPI

"I have seen many magnificent tables, with beautiful flowers, the finest porcelain, amazing silverware, but alas the glasses are never of the same caliber." Thus Alessandro Zoppi, Venetian collector of antique Murano glasses, describes the place of central importance that he accords in the arts of the table to these everyday objects. In his palazzo on the Grand Canal, one of the rare private residences to have frescoes by Tiepolo, he has assembled an exceptional collection covering over three hundred years of the history of glassmaking, from eighteenth-century pieces to contemporary designs by Zecchin, Martinuzzi, and Scarpa. Not even the owners themselves know how many wonders this treasure trove contains!

FACING PAGE AND RIGHT
The centerpiece of Roberta Rossi's table is a magnificent creation by Seguso, set on a Burano lace tablecloth. The dining room is lined with Fortuny fabric and decorated in a chinoiserie-inspired style.

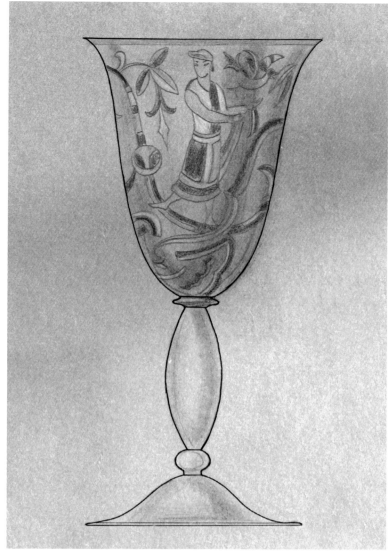

FACING PAGE
Rods of colored, opaque, and transparent glass, made in the Murano workshops, are cut and heated to be worked by the glassblowers.

ABOVE LEFT
Detail of a table bouquet in colored glass.

ABOVE RIGHT
Design for a glass with a figurative motif (S.A.L.I.R. collection).

FABRIC AND LACE

MONOPOLIES ON GOLD
THREAD AND SILK

China's age-old monopoly on silk came to an end in the sixth century, when Emperor Justinian had some silkworm cocoons smuggled back to Byzantium. With its close links with the Byzantine Empire, Venice was soon able to buy some of these cocoons and to start manufacturing raw silk. As early as the eleventh century, the Venetians were known for "the art of silk fabrics woven with gold and silver." The exclusive preserve of women, this was a more complex form of weaving in which the silk was enriched with precious metallic threads, initially of pure gold and then, from the thirteenth century to the sixteenth, silver that was sometimes gilded. Marco Polo has left us magnificent descriptions of Venetians decked out in sumptuous cloth of gold.

In the thirteenth century, velvet and the *velluderi*, or velvet weavers, made their first appearance in Venice. Velvet, which had its own unit of measurement, the *coble*, was subject, like glass, to strict legislation. In 1366, the Venetian Republic prohibited its manufacture outside the city, and set up a commission to control the making of silk and the manufacturing processes for producing the different colors, including the famous scarlet. Venetian fabrics reached their peak of magnificence in the fourteenth century, when the export trade attained new heights. The *alto e basso*, or pile-on-pile, technique was invented, and the fantastical motifs of the previous century, featuring dragons and an imaginary bestiary, gave way to patterns of floral motifs, pomegranates, and pine cones. Sumptuary laws notwithstanding, opulent fabrics invaded every sphere: interiors, dress, and liturgical vestments. The restrictions imposed by the Republic were severe, nonetheless. In 1476, a decree was issued banning cushions embellished with precious stones, and in 1490 another decree forbade

Venetians from wearing any cloth of gold or silver that had not been woven in Venice.

The fifteenth century saw the development of lighter fabrics, such as damask and brocatelle, that were used to line the walls of palazzo interiors. it became the custom among patrician circles to name the rooms in their residences the "Gold Room" or "Tapestry Room" after the fabrics that covered their walls. The Palazzo Pisani, which now houses the Conservatory of Music, still has its *Stanza d'oro* (Gold Room). The seventeenth century drew a dividing line between fabrics intended for clothing and those reserved for soft furnishings. The fabrics used to line the walls of a room were chosen to match the furniture, stucco decorations, and paintings. But decline was not far off, sealed notably by competition from the French and Colbert's protectionist policies, which offered greater freedom in the weight and quality of the raw materials used.

From the end of the Republic to the Austro-Hungarian Empire and the creation of the Kingdom of Italy, Venice suffered a period of great poverty. With economic recovery came the establishment of the Venetian cotton mills, Cotoneficio Veneziano, in 1883. Velvet, which had almost been consigned to oblivion, was revived in 1858 thanks to two companies, Sartori and Trapolin, which became Bevilacqua and Rubelli. These two firms, specialists in the reproduction of fabrics from the era of the Venetian Republic, developed artistic collaborations with great names such as the artists Guido Cadorin and Vittorio Zecchin. The excellence of Venetian fabrics survives to this day in the historic center of Venice, thanks to the famous workshops of Bevilacqua and Fortuny.

FORTUNY

The brilliant Spanish-born designer Mariano Fortuny revolutionized the art of Venetian textiles in the early twentieth century. Drawing on historical sources and thoroughly grounded in a knowledge of all things oriental and of the antique fabrics that his father collected, in 1907 he set up a workshop for printed fabrics, linked initially with his theatrical activities and stage designs. Using stencils or *katagami*, Fortuny designed original combinations of oriental and Japanese motifs, and in 1910 he patented a printing system based on silk-screen printing applied in a continuous strip. This he applied to silk, silk velvet, and airy voiles for the theater, and to cotton velvet and cotton decorated with large Renaissance-style motifs for interior decoration. From 1911, he showed his work at the Salon des Arts Décoratifs in Paris.

Fortuny had a magical ability to imbue his fabrics with the spirit of the times. In early twentieth-century Venice, the atmosphere was electric with the decadence of D'Annunzio, the Ballets Russes,

and Isadora Duncan. Clothes became simpler and purer in style, inspired by classical Greece and the tunic of the Charioteer of Delphi. The timeless Delphos gown and Knossos scarf were born, decorated with gold motifs inspired by a Hellenistic vocabulary. In 1909, Fortuny registered the patent for pleated silk. His talents were even celebrated by Proust: "The Fortuny dress Albertine wore that evening seemed to me like the seductive shadow of that invisible Venice. It was invaded by Arabic ornamentation, like Venice."

In 1919, on the advice of Giancarlo Stucky, Fortuny opened a printed fabric factory on the island of La Giudecca. On his death in 1949, the factory was taken over by the American interior designer Elsie McNeill Lee, Countess Gozzi, his friend and pupil who was ambassador for the brand for forty years. The factory is now owned by the Riad family, and under Alberto Torsello continues to produce the magnificent fabrics that are so celebrated throughout the world.

PAGES 200–201
The Fortuny showroom today.
The design studio is still off
limits to visitors.
FACING PAGE AND RIGHT
Details of Elsie McNeill's house.
ABOVE
In this early twentieth-century
photograph, Idea and Menotti
Beffagna wear Fortuny
designs (private collection).
Initially a seamstress, Idea later
became the platonic model
for the artist's designs.

"All that was proposed appears to have been the enrichment of surface, so as to make it delightful to the eye; and this being once understood, a decorated piece of marble became to the architect just what a piece of lace or embroidery is to a dressmaker." **JOHN RUSKIN,** *The Stones of Venice,* 1851.

ABOVE AND FACING PAGE
A room hung with antique cloth of gold in the Palazzo Bernardo and the Bevilacqua fabric in a green and gold colorway chosen by the owner.

**ABOVE, FACING PAGE,
AND PAGES 208–209**
The subtle refinement
of the Palazzo Bernardo
interiors with antique fabrics
of different eras, including
some by Rubelli.

LEFT, FACING PAGE, AND PAGES 212–13
Antique Bevilacqua fabrics lend the Palazzo Polignac a typically Venetian atmosphere.

LEFT
Carlos de Beistegui's bed,
Palazzo Polignac. In 1964,
Beistegui sold the Palazzo
Labia and parted with its
furniture in a memorable sale
described by Paul Morand:
"Beneath [his] ivory hammer,
the whole life of a collector
vanished into thin air."
Bought by the Palazzo
Polignac, Beistegui's
sixteen-foot (five-meter)
tester bed, in yellow
Bevilacqua silk embroidered
with antique tassels and
fringes, is now the central
feature of one of the
bedrooms on the piano
nobile.

BEVILACQUA

Founded in 1800, Luigi Bevilacqua's weaving
workshop soon became famous for its art fabrics
inspired by historical models and the use of
the perforated cards invented by Joseph Marie
Jacquard in 1801. In 1895, Ernesto Trevisani
observed that the firm was "famous for its brocades
and damasks of excellent quality and taste."

   With over three thousand designs, the firm's
historical archives are an inexhaustible source of
inspiration, enabling it to launch new collections
every year and to bring historical models back into
production. The Bevilacqua workshop and eighteen
hand looms, dating back to the eighteenth century
and still in operation today, produce sumptuous cut
velvets and resplendent brocades woven using
traditional Venetian technical expertise.

BELOW AND FACING PAGE
The Bevilacqua workshop,
with its wooden looms and
its archives, encapsulates
a whole legacy of an
outstanding traditional
expertise.

FACING PAGE AND RIGHT
An eighteenth-century loom.
Working by hand means only
a limited amount of fabric
can be produced per day,
making the finished piece
all the more extraordinary.
ABOVE
Multicolored silk threads
promise future splendors.
Up to fifteen thousand
threads may be used in
a single design.

ABOVE LEFT
The entrance to the
Bevilacqua showroom.

ABOVE RIGHT
All the wealth of the archives
is concentrated in these
antique perforated cards,
representing so many
different patterns to be
reproduced on the Jacquard
looms.

FACING PAGE
Bevilacqua fabrics are
renowned internationally
for their exquisite quality.
They do not exceed
24 in. (60 cm) in width,
the maximum size allowed
by the hand looms.

LEFT
One of Philippe Starck's most recent designs for Bevilacqua now lines the walls of the Grancaffè Quadri on St. Mark's Square. In a humorous twist, it features the faces of the managers, the Alajmo brothers, instead of the original Gorgon heads, in a "grotesque"-style brocade with floral motif.
FACING PAGE
Portrait of Raffaele Alajmo.

LACE: SEA FOAM FROM BURANO

Although Venice cannot claim with any certainty to have invented lace, it is its cradle and home par excellence. Legend has it that the first lace, a veil born of air and sea foam, was given by a mermaid to a poor Burano fisherman as a wedding gift for his bride. The historical origins of lace remain uncertain, but the first pieces were certainly produced in waterside villages, thanks to the skill of fishermen's wives in repairing the fishing nets and their dexterity with needle and thread. Lacemakers were invariably the wives, sisters, or daughters of fishermen.

In the sixteenth century, to meet a growing demand for lace, Dogaressa Morosina Morosini, wife of Doge Grimani, founded the first lace workshop in Venice, with one hundred and thirty lacemakers. Organized production began in Burano, where the famous "stitch in air" gained such fame and magnificence that in the seventeenth century sumptuary laws banned it, on pain of a fine of two hundred ducats. The "Venezia," "rosette," and "Burano" stitches that appeared at this time were prized throughout Europe. Colbert brought over two hundred Venetian lacemakers to France to teach their art, particularly in Alençon. Bobbin lace was also a Venetian specialty, flourishing until the fall of the Republic.

After this, lace production declined until the mid-nineteenth century, when two separate figures quite independently saved this age-old tradition from disappearing. In 1872, Andriana Marcello, a lady-in-waiting to Queen Margherita of Savoy, established the Burano Lace School, founded on the priceless teaching of the last lacemaker, Cencia Scarpariola, then seventy years old. Accepting up to four hundred apprentices in its heyday, the school closed its doors in 1970. In Pellestrina, meanwhile, Michelangelo Jesurum founded a school specializing in bobbin lace, where over five thousand lacemakers and embroiderers were employed. One of his inventions, polychrome lace, was awarded a gold medal at the Paris Universal Exhibition in 1878.

In the twentieth century, Olga Asta, the sign of whose famous lace shop can still be seen on St. Mark's Square, was one of the last businesswomen to put her faith in this exceptional craft. Changing fashions, and the cost and time-consuming nature of the work, have put an end to lace production on a major scale in Burano. But perhaps one day the sleeping beauty may awaken...

FACING PAGE, ABOVE, AND PAGES 226–27
On this table spread with a Burano lace tablecloth, the napkins are embroidered with the *corno dogale*, the famous cap worn by the doges of Venice (Frigerio Zeno family collection).

"The Queen ... was blonde and rosy, and her face was lighted by her ever-ready smile, as she looked out from the cloud of creamy Buranesi laces.... Beside her sat Andriana Duodo where, on that industrious island, she cultivated flax, and raised the most marvelous old-fashioned flowers." GABRIELE D'ANNUNZIO, *The Flame*, 1900.

PAGES 228–29
The christening gown made for Maria Teresa Zeno at the beginning of the twentieth century using precious fragments of antique Burano lace has been passed down from generation to generation in this Venetian family (Frigerio Zeno family collection). Given that it takes the lacemakers over two months to embroider a small handkerchief on their *tombolo*, the small cylindrical cushion they use as a support, the amount of work involved in this delicate creation is hard to imagine.

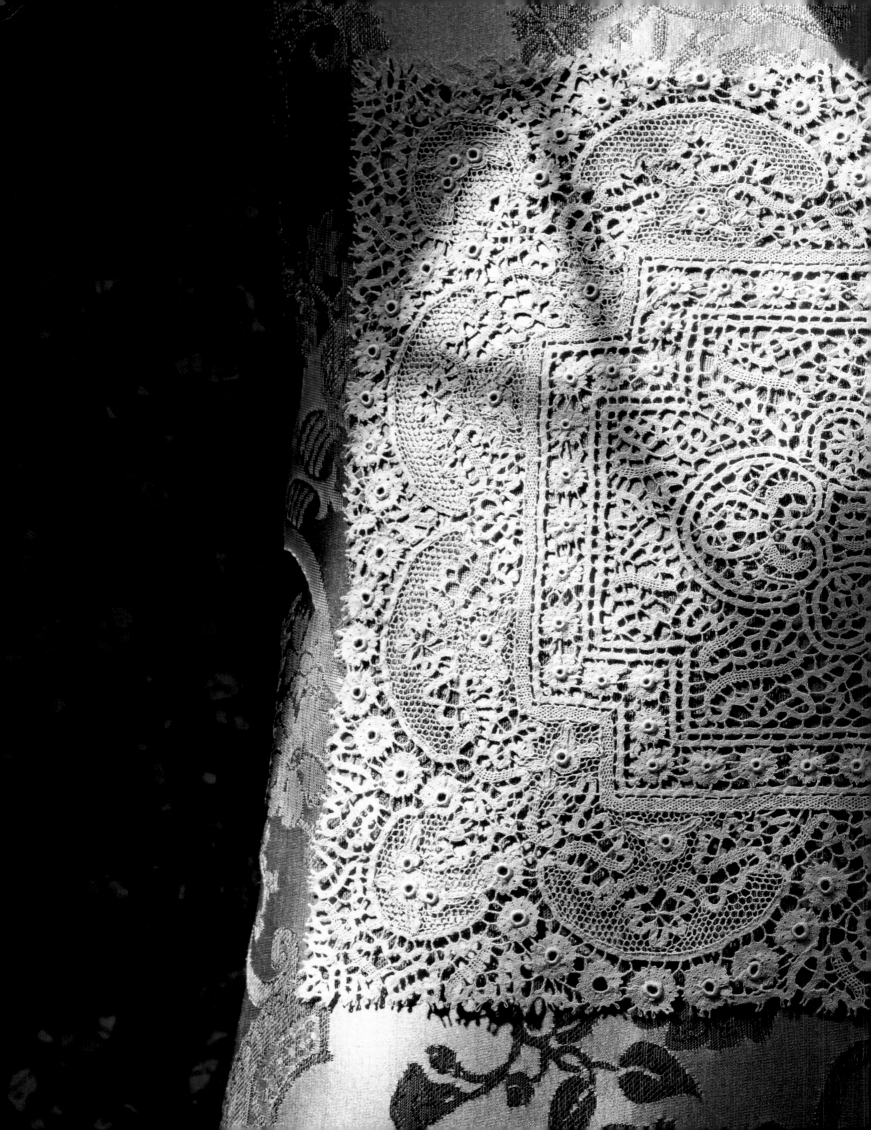

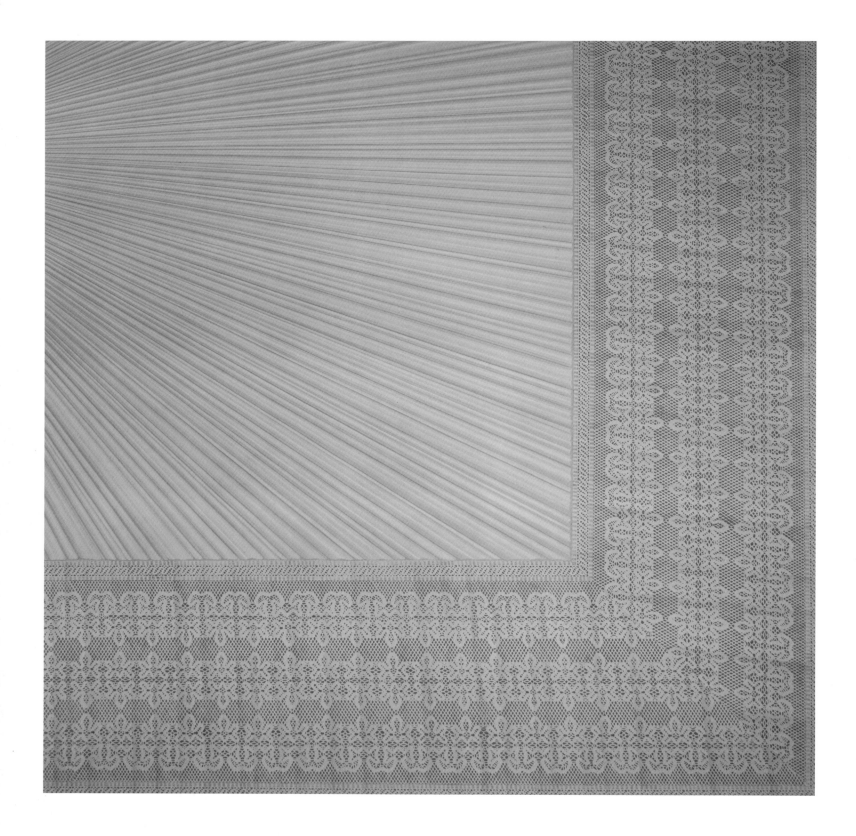

PAGES 230–31
Lace from Olga Asta's
famous shop, now closed but
with its sign still visible on
St. Mark's Square (Stella Asta
collection). Although not
a lacemaker herself, Olga
excelled in the creation of
bridal veils and trousseaux,
tablecloths, napkins,
and sheets.

ABOVE AND FACING PAGE
An extraordinary
trompe-l'œil lace ceiling
in the Palazzo Loredan
dell'Ambasciatore.

CERAMICS AND PORCELAIN

Perhaps more than any other material, porcelain embodied the spirit of the eighteenth century. Light and elegant, it lent itself to the creation of dazzling objets d'art, to the point of being dubbed "white gold." The formula for the creation of porcelain, long kept secret by China, was imported to Europe by the court of Augustus the Strong, King of Poland, and quickly spread throughout Europe. The Republic of Venice was the first European state to possess four porcelain factories. The Venetian porcelain collections—one of the least familiar of the Venetian arts—are preserved in the museum housed in the Ca' Rezzonico.

The dominance of the glass industry has gradually tended to overshadow the fact that a corporation of ceramicists known as *bochaleri* existed in the city as early as 1500, to disappear in the aftermath of the Napoleonic era. The lagoon is still full of shards of old majolica, since it was the custom to use the porcelain waste to consolidate the banks—as may easily be seen from passing boats at low tide.

In the eighteenth century, at least three private hard-paste porcelain factories, Vezzi, Hewelcke, and, later, Cozzi, ensured that Venice became the second European state after Saxony to have its own production. The first of these, opened in 1720 by Giovanni Vezzi with Christopher Hunger, an Austrian, was in operation for only seven years—seven difficult years since one of the imported raw materials, kaolin, had to be smuggled in. A few decades later, in 1764, the factory set up by Geminiano Cozzi solved this problem by using Italian kaolin from Tretto.

The famous red anchor, the mark of Cozzi porcelain, paid symbolic tribute to Venice's maritime history. Famed for his floral pieces and decorative chinoiserie, Cozzi also created figurative designs dubbed *a bersò* in the Venetian dialect, featuring predominantly green scenes of flower beds, topiary, and pergolas in the gardens of Venetian villas. Closed in 1799, the Cozzi name has recently been reborn, reproducing the firm's historical designs alongside new creations.

Among twentieth-century Venetian ceramics, which are highly sought after by collectors, one of the most entertaining was San Polo, which took its name from the campo where it was established in 1947. One of the most famous collaborators on its modern ceramics inspired by the commedia dell'arte subjects—Harlequins and Pulcinellas in vivid colors and gondolier stripes—was the artist Otello Rosa. The factory closed in 1959, but its output, mainly of lamps, vases, and sculptures, remains highly prized.

FACING PAGE AND PAGES 236–37
The large table in Marta Bastianello's dining room (see p. 269), spread with an Arjumand tablecloth from Bologna on which are arranged a set of antique glasses decorated with fine gold (Murano, eighteenth century), typically Venetian silver cutlery (San Marco, nineteenth century), and eighteenth-century majolica plates with tacchiolo decoration from the Antonibon factory at Nove near Bassano.

RIGHT
Marta Bastianello's
dining room.

LEFT AND FACING PAGE
A more intimate table in Marta Bastianello's home, in front of the Matthias Schaller photograph *Controfacciata, Palazzo Mocenigo*. On the tablecloth by Chiarastella Cattana, the fish plates are Ginori porcelain (mid-nineteenth century), and the Venini filigree glasses with square bases are by Tomaso Buzzi (1933).

FACING PAGE, RIGHT, AND PAGES 242–43
A collection of twentieth-century San Polo ceramics (Venice, private collection). Modern and cheerful, their bright colors and stripes evoke the commedia dell'arte and gondoliers.

STUCCO

FACING PAGE AND PAGES 246-47
Details of the stucco decorations in the Casa Cicogna. In 1950, Contessa Anna Maria Cicogna Mozzoni Volpi bought a beautiful abandoned palazzo near the Basilica of Santa Maria della Salute, and entrusted its refurbishment to the surrealist set designer, painter, and architect Fabrizio Clerici.
In collaboration with artists, including Andrea Spadini and Fabius von Gugel, he created a home that is unique of its type, one of the last palazzi in the twentieth century to be decorated with stucco throughout.

Stucco remains one of the most undervalued of skilled crafts. Not quite a major art, nor yet a minor one either, stucco seems to be erased from official accounts as though condemned by *damnatio memoriae*. Immanuel Kant even went so far as to describe it as *Schmuck*, a useless ornament, superfluous, and faux because it obscured a building's structure. But in Venice, stucco hits you between the eyes. White, gilded, or colored, it forms an integral part of the city.

The origins of stucco stretch back to antiquity, in painted decorations in Crete, Malta, and Egypt, some dating back over three millennia. It varies in composition, but always contains an aggregate such as plaster or powdered marble or stone, and a binder in the form of lime or cement. Unlike plaster molds, which can be mass-produced, in stucco the artist works directly on the decorations of ceilings or walls, using a remarkable degree of technical skill, since the modeling depends on the drying time and the material used. Sculptures in stucco are lighter and softer than those in plaster. Stucco was widely used in ancient Rome; in *De Architectura* Vitruvius made reference to the preparation of *marmorino*, which was used to cover Roman houses with plant motifs, cornucopias, and a variety of figures. Later, in the sixteenth century, Rome also saw the introduction of two important decorative innovations, when the architect Giacomo Barozzi da Vignola introduced the use of white and gilded stucco and Antonio Tempesta introduced the human figure.

From as early as the sixteenth century, Venice had its own masters, Venetians either by birth or adoption, since they often came from Lombardy and Ticino but were trained in the Republic's workshops. The important stucco artist Alessandro Vittoria trained in the workshop of Jacopo Sansovino and worked with Palladio on the stuccowork of the Doges' Palace between 1559 and 1567. In his work may be seen the first signs of the flouting of the classical canon and the premises of the quest for a new aesthetic in the baroque era.

In the sixteenth century, the explosion of the baroque saw the consecration of stucco. Abbondio Stazio and Carpoforo Tencalla decorated the finest palazzi of this period with putti and decorative entrelacs respectively. Perfect examples of their work can be seen on the Palazzo Albrizzi, Palazzo Barbaro, and Ca' Zenobio. The seventeenth century's abhorrence of a vacuum loaded houses, palazzi, and churches with a wealth of white and gilded stucco, while the rococo period colored stucco pink, violet, pale gray, or yellow, and it now embellished smaller spaces such as mezzanines or ground floors, as may be seen in Giuseppe Ferrari's decorations of the mezzanine of the Palazzo Pisani. The eighteenth century saw the apotheosis of Venetian *marmorino* in this unique rococo style.

The neoclassical period rediscovered a more polished style, with the emphasis on elegance and sobriety. Gian Antonio Selva created the stucco ornamentation for La Fenice Opera House and the private Palazzo Smith Mangili Valmarana. But with the nineteenth century came the first signs of decline, and soon new fashions in interior decoration—including draperies, silks, painted finishes, wallpaper, and plasterboard—would swallow up stucco completely.

**ABOVE, FACING PAGE,
AND PAGE 251**
Stucco on the ceiling
and walls of the staircase
at the Casa Cicogna:
sinuous foliate decorations
on a monumental scale.
PAGE 250
An elegant stucco trophy on
a wall in the Palazzo Polignac.

FACING PAGE AND RIGHT
Stucco bas-reliefs in
the Palazzo Papadopoli.

FACING PAGE
In the Palazzo Frigerio Zeno, circular mirrors with opulent stucco frames reflect each other to create illusory perspectives.

ABOVE
Views and details of the palazzo belonging to Martina Luccarda.

IN PURSUIT
OF THE
EXTRAORDINARY

THE BIENNALE

In 1895, the creation of the Biennale, an event for contemporary art, dance, music, architecture, and, later (in 1932), cinema, gave Venice a new lease of life, and an alternative attraction to its historical treasures. In 1903, a new section dedicated to the decorative arts was opened up to makers of glass, lace, textiles, and ceramics. Although the painter Ettore Tito presented the first collaboration between an artist and the glass masters of Murano in 1905, glass did not become a major presence until 1910, since Murano was too busy developing its prolific trade in glass mosaic. Already famous thanks to the basilicas of Torcello and San Marco and popularized by John Ruskin, glass mosaic tiles began to invade private homes and even the Biennale itself, when, in 1928, its bar was entirely sheathed in glass mosaic by the architect Brenno del Giudice. The sales report for the exhibition of 1912 gives an idea of the position occupied by the decorative arts: 303 paintings and 26 sculptures were sold, alongside 302 objets d'art, including 106 pieces in glass.

After World War I, fresh impetus was given by Vittorio Zecchin, a figure of major importance in the Venetian decorative arts. Born among the glassmakers of Murano, Zecchin was a painter, a passionate interior designer, and a promoter of the arts and crafts. Aware of the importance of a strong local production intended for the international market, he presented tapestries at the Biennale in 1922, lace in 1930, bouclé damasks for Rubelli in 1934, and, most importantly, works in glass when he became artistic director of Cappelin-Venini. "The combination of Cappelin's taste, Venini's business sense, and Zecchin's knowledge of glass techniques were to create the most revolutionary trio in Murano glass design in the first half of the twentieth century," summarizes Cristina Beltrami. From an island of glassmakers, Murano became an island of designers. In 1932, the decorative section had its own space in the Biennale gardens, in the aptly named Venezia Pavilion, strongly supported by Giuseppe Volpi.

In 1948, the first postwar Biennale, the event confirmed its leading role as one of the most prestigious international art events, presenting for the first time the collection of a certain Peggy Guggenheim. Sadly, the closure of the sales offices in 1970, followed two years later by that of the decorative arts pavilion, marked the end of any artistic collaborations with master glassmakers at the Biennale, so signing, in David Landau's words, "the death warrant of Murano." But Venice continues to inspire artists. For some years now, painters, sculptors, architects, interior designers, writers, and musicians, all of them Venetians by birth or adoption, have been breathing new life into the Venetian arts and crafts scene.

RIGHT
A selection of designs
presented during the last
exhibition in the Decorative
Arts Pavilion at the 1972
Biennale: Merletti vases in
opalescent glass by Thorssen
& Karlsson for Venini & Cie
(private collection).

ARCHITECTS AND INTERIOR DESIGNERS
UMBERTO BRANCHINI

The great art of an interior designer often consists in drawing attention away from the successive occupancies of and changes to a house over time and endowing it with its own personality, while at the same respecting its history. This presented a challenge on a major scale for Umberto Branchini, whose Venetian home, originally a convent, had been subjected to an architectonic intervention by a famous architect in the 1960s. The salon, with its lofty ceilings and air of sanctity, offers an ideal setting for Umberto Branchini's furniture designs, making a lighthearted mix of the past and the future. An artistic director and interior designer born in Lombardy, Branchini has been living and working in Venice for over twenty years, starting out as a sculptor before he developed a passion for design and interior decoration. Displayed on the Calo Scarpa Doge table in the dining room are miniature models of his latest furniture designs: the Palline coffee table with its patina recalling the ebbing tide, and the Courtisane couch referencing Veronica Franco, the famous poet and courtesan who founded the convent in the sixteenth-century. These evocative names pay homage to the city that has welcomed him.

FACING PAGE AND ABOVE LEFT
The grandiose former
convent interior serves
as a dramatic setting
for the living area.
ABOVE RIGHT
Portrait of
Umberto Branchini.

**PAGES 264–65, LEFT,
AND FACING PAGE**
The uncluttered simplicity
of the private rooms in
Umberto Branchini's home
contrasts with the historic
grandeur of the reception
spaces.

MARTA BASTIANELLO

"Growing up in Venice is a privilege that has a profound effect and leaves its mark on you," says Marta Bastianello. In her apartment on the Grand Canal, this architect—Venetian by birth, Milanese by adoption—mixes the styles of the two cities she loves so much. Respectful of the historical background of her apartment, she gives expression to her more contemporary tastes through her passion for the decorative arts. Her husband, Cesare, is the nephew of the architect and interior designer Tomaso Buzzi, one of twentieth-century Italy's leading designers who was also the artistic director of Venini from 1932 to 1934. His work is recalled in the Venini lamps in the bathroom and the glasses with filigree and very modern-looking square stems. For years the pair have been great aficionados of the work of Venetian artists and craftsmen, collecting ceramics from all periods. Both have their favorites: Bassano, Nove, and Antonibon for Marta; Cozzi and the Milanese Clerici and Rubati for Cesare.

FACING PAGE
Marta Bastianello and Cesare Buzzi Ferraris' mirror room.
ABOVE LEFT
Architect Marta Bastianello at home.
ABOVE RIGHT
The architect combined a mirror framed with intricate baroque curves with a wallpaper by Elena Carozzi.

ARCHITECTS AND INTERIOR DESIGNERS
MATTEO AND SUSANNE THUN

In their Venetian bolt-hole, Matteo and Susanne Thun have brought together their favorite pieces in glass—glass is an indissoluble link between the famous designer-architect and the city. On the table and the bookshelves are iconic works created by the Memphis Group. Founded in Milan in 1981, this Italian design collective, whose members included Matteo Thun, Ettore Sottsass, Aldo Cibic, Matteo Zanini, Shiro Kuramata, and Michael Graves, pioneered postmodernism in the 1980s. Their signature style, featuring the use of plastic materials in bright and often clashing colors, has been likened to the advent of Technicolor or the art of Roy Lichtenstein.

In 1986, Ettore Sottsass obtained the authorization of the master glassmakers of Murano to modify their manufacturing regulations to use chemical glue rather than heat in the traditional way. This revolutionary technique opened the way to a new creative impulse and a series of pieces with Greek names: Amaltea, Astimelusa, Erinna, Imera, Ananke, Clesitera, Parsifalia, and Clinira.

BELOW AND FACING PAGE
On the Tartare table,
the Niobe vase in blown glass
by Ettore Sottsass, 1986.
On the bookshelves, Bolle,
the best-known series
by designer Tapio Wirkkala,
created between 1966
and 1967 for Venini.

PAINTERS AND SCULPTORS
GIGI BON

Between 1438 and 1442, the Venetian sculptor Giovanni Bon created a flamboyant Gothic masterpiece for the façade of the Doges' Palace, the famous Porta della Carta. The altar in the Mascoli Chapel in St. Mark's Basilica is also attributed to him. Today, Gigi Bon lives just a few meters from the basilica. Same initials, same family name, same profession. This Venetian sculptor finds a constant source of inspiration in the Serenissima. Her work, created in bronze using the lost wax process, bears the imprint of surrealism and resembles a celestial alchemy between sky and sea. Creatures emerging from the fathomless depths of the lagoon, signs of the Zodiac, corals, and fossils decorate the works conceived and preserved in this silent inner sanctum. Like a Renaissance cabinet of curiosities, or *Wunderkammer*, this timeless atelier is filled with mirabilia combining the unfamiliar, the mysterious, and the fantastical.

"Say 'Venice,' and you seem to hear glass breaking under the silence of the moon ... 'Venice,' and it is like a silken fabric tearing in a shaft of sunlight ... 'Venice,' and all the colors mingle in an ever-changing transparency ... Is it not a place of enchantment, magic, and illusion?"

HENRI DE RÉGNIER, "Esquisses vénitiennes," *La Revue de Paris*, 1905.

LEFT
For Gigi Bon, "Art is a quest through history, time, and nature; bronze is the image of eternity." Her sculptures are imaginary beasts, allegories of a timeless Venice.
FACING PAGE
A fascinating cabinet of curiosities with a strangeness that is uniquely Venetian, Gigi Bon's studio is testimony to the culture of an artist who is also a collector and bibliophile.

"Undulating on the broad expanse of the canal you see the steady or whitish forms of the palazzi, slumbering in the cool and silence of the dawn; you forget everything, your career, your plans, yourself; you gaze, you gather, you savor, as though quite suddenly, released from life, airborne, you were floating above it all, in the light and the azure skies."

HIPPOLYTE TAINE, *Venice*, 1864.

PAINTERS AND SCULPTORS
DAVIDE BATTISTIN

Born in Venice in 1970, Davide Battistin graduated from the Accademia di Belle Arti in Venice in 1998. His paintings explore the light of his native city and its effects at different times of the day on the lagoon, the canals, and the palazzo façades. Horizons stretching to infinity, sunsets, and mysterious mists are constantly refined, creating uniquely Venetian impressions, sensations, and emotions captured on canvas like dreams. Davide Battistin in Dorsoduro, historically the quarter of artists and writers.

FACING PAGE
Davide Battistin, painter of the Venetian light, at home in front of one of his paintings.

LEFT AND FACING PAGE, TOP
On the table designed
by Carlo Scarpa, a sculpture
by Pierre Charpin stands
alongside arrows by
G. William Webb and a
pumpkin by Giovanni Rizzoli.
FACING PAGE BOTTOM
Karole Vail and Andrew
Huston: art as legacy.
PAGES 282–83
Karole Vail and Andrew
Huston's living room under
the eaves.

PAINTERS AND SCULPTORS
KAROLE VAIL AND ANDREW HUSTON

It's hard not to feel an innate connection with Venice when you are the granddaughter of one of its icons, Peggy Guggenheim. Director of the Peggy Guggenheim Collection in Venice since 2017, Karole Vail has returned to her family roots after living for years in New York with her husband, the British artist Andrew Huston. "It's wonderful to come back not as her granddaughter but as director of the collection, and not to sleep in a room lined with surrealist paintings anymore," she jokes. Her grandmother loved to discover and promote local artists, whom she often encountered in the All'Angelo restaurant, such as Emilio Vedova and Tancredi. It is a family passion. In their Venetian apartment, the couple display their shared love of art through modern and contemporary paintings by artist friends, and by Andrew's works inspired by the shifting Venetian tides, as in his evocative *Tides and Arches* series. He has a studio on the ground floor of the magnificent Palazzo Polignac, and he regularly rows out into the lagoon he loves so much to explore its colors and capture them in his paintings and sculptures.

PAINTERS AND SCULPTORS
ROGER DE MONTEBELLO

What finer inspiration could an artist wish for than studio windows
overlooking the Basilica of La Salute? Here the French painter
Roger de Montebello finds one of his favorite themes: views of
the urban fabric of Venice depicted with architectural precision.
For Montebello, Venice is a world in itself, self-sufficient, a world
where everything is echoed in a perfect mirror, in reflections on water.
His paintings of classical architecture seem to float in an abstract
universe. Church portals and the Punta della Dogana in the mists
of day or night are among his favorite subjects. He is often
to be found in the *calle* of Venice, his paintbox on his knees,
in search of the perfect light.

ABOVE
A studio with a view. Roger
de Montebello in front
of his subject, the Basilica of
Santa Maria della Salute.
FACING PAGE
The breathtaking panorama
of the Grand Canal from
the studio windows,
like a veduta of Venice.
PAGES 286–87
Roger de Montebello's studio.

COLLECTORS
CRISTINA AND INTI LIGABUE

One of the most original and interesting of all Venetian institutions, the Ligabue Foundation encourages the fostering of research and knowledge in the fields of archaeology, anthropology, and the natural sciences—subjects not usually associated with Venice—through thematic exhibitions. The foundation also preserves the collections of Inti's father, Giancarlo Ligabue, heir to the Ligabue company, specialist food suppliers to ships and oil rigs for almost a hundred years. An explorer, collector, and researcher, a true Indiana Jones of the lagoon, Giancarlo Ligabue presented the Museum of Natural History in Venice with its first complete fossil dinosaur skeleton, *Ouranosaurus nigeriensis*, discovered on an expedition in 1972, and a reptile skull weighing several hundred kilos. From an early age, Inti followed his father on his expeditions, and in turn developed a passion for ethnography and the study of civilizations and tribes around the world.

FACING PAGE
With his wife Cristina, Inti Ligabue has been organizing themed exhibitions since 2016. Together they cultivate a very Venetian *art de vivre*, notably with the big celebration they throw in September ever year for the Regata Storica.
ABOVE
Inti Ligabue keeps the objects that are dearest to him in his family palazzo overlooking the Grand Canal.

SECRET GARDENS

In this city on the water, where every square foot of land is hard won from the lagoon, the very idea of a garden is a treasure so miraculous that almost seems unreal. In the seventeenth century, a precise inventory of the gardens in each district was drawn up, moreover. But in addition to the five hundred or so gardens listed in the city, the palazzi of Venice conceal private entrances and secret courtyards, places of mystery hidden away from the outside world, and merely glimpsed here and there through sculpted portals and elaborately worked gates. The palazzi on the Grand Canal have pontoons for arrivals by boat, but in addition they also have one or more street entrances, hidden from view. These internal courtyards form evocative settings that enhance the magic of Venetian palazzo architecture. Havens of calm, contemplation, and meditation, these secret spaces embody an *art de vivre* imbued with beauty in its daily life and a gentle sweetness in its intimacy. As everywhere in Venice, the plants here are all climbers—vines, ivies, roses, and wisterias—vying with each other to reach up to the sky, like the terraces and *altane* perched on the palazzo roofs.

Gardens on the island of La Giudecca are more spacious, and one of the largest private gardens, laid out around the Fortuny factory, has invited us in. Elsie McNeill Lee, Mario Fortuny's friend and collaborator, who took over the factory after his death in 1949, had it laid out as a landscape garden, even endowing it with a swimming pool—for many years the only private pool in Venice. Designed around the preserved remains of the convent that once stood on the site, this spacious garden is a haven of peace and inspiration. It also forms an ideal counterpoint to the intense manufacturing activity in the famous red brick building, with its unmissable name spelt out in large white letters.

FACING PAGE
The narrow tree-lined path leading to Palazzo Bernardo forms a magical space, fragrant with the scent of orange trees.

"[W]hile the golden hours elapsed and the plants drank in the light and the inscrutable old palace turned pale and then, as the day waned, began to flush." **HENRY JAMES,** *The Aspern Papers*, 1888.

FACING PAGE
A typically Venetian internal courtyard, with wellhead, steps, and large Gothic windows forming a theatrical setting worthy of Shakespeare.
RIGHT
A bas-relief of the lion of St. Mark, emblem of the Serenissima, on the brick walls enclosing the gardens of the Fortuny factory.

LEFT AND PAGES 296–97
The gardens surrounding
the Fortuny factory on
La Giudecca enjoy the luxury
of space. The *cortile* retains
the wellhead of the former
convent as its central feature,
before opening out into a
superb ornamental garden.
FACING PAGE
A fountain with the head
of a faun.

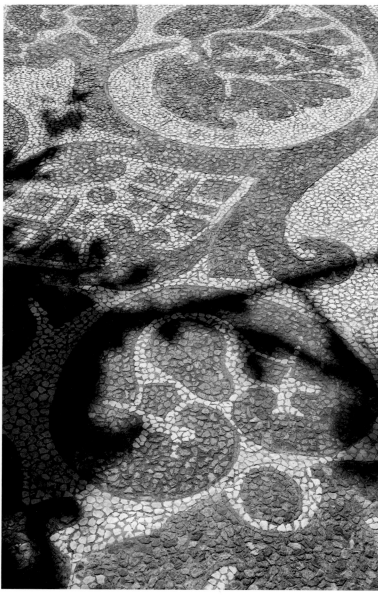

ABOVE, FACING PAGE,
AND PAGES 300–301
The small internal courtyard
of the Casa Cicogna, with
a modern take on the classic
combination of a stone
bench, here a dazzling
rendition of daybed,
and a row of caryatids,
here languid, sylph-like, and
unmistakably surrealist.

VENICE: A PRIVATE INVITATION

298

FACING PAGE
A quiet spot in the privacy
of a Venetian terrace garden.
ABOVE
A wisteria grows in luxuriant
profusion over the brick walls
surrounding a historic home.
Doorways with graceful
architectural details and
delicate wrought-iron gates
hold out the promise of
the beauties to be found in
the Venetian palazzi within.

ACKNOWLEDGMENTS

Many thanks to all the Venetians who have welcomed me into their city, their homes, and above all into their family histories, testimonies to an exceptional *art de vivre*.

Thank you to my Venetian husband, Giovanni Giol, without whom the Venice presented in this book would probably never have opened its doors to me.
My gratitude goes to Pierre Passebon for organizing that delightful meeting with Suzanne Tise-Isoré from which the idea for this book was born.
Grazie to Luca De Michelis and Emanuela Bassetti, my Italian publishers.
My deepest thanks to Pierre Rosenberg for taking the time to write the preface to this book; Pierre has been a Venetian for longer than I have and his insight is invaluable. Thank you, too to his wife, Beatrice, for her discreet support.
I am truly grateful to all of my friends, Giberto Arrivabene, Marta Bastianello, Gigi Bon, Giorgio Ceccato, Matteo Corvino, Chahan Minassian, Alberto Torsello, Cathy Vedovi, for taking the time to dress their tables, each more beautiful than the last, each with its own theme and its own character.

This book would not have been the same without two exceptional private archives, indispensable for an understanding of the way life was lived in the twentieth century: the Arrivabene archives of Giberto and Bianca Arrivabene, with its century of women and extraordinary parties and celebrations; and the Frigerio Zeno archives of Nicolò and Elena Frigerio Zeno, a mine of information on the daily purchases made by Venetian ladies around St. Mark's Square, and all the small crafts and trades that have now disappeared.

My heartfelt thanks go to the following:
– Marino Barovier and David Landau
for re-creating for us the last glass table—historic and extremely rare — exhibited at the 1972 Biennale of the Decorative Arts.
– Catherine Buyse Dian, Jean-Marie Degueldre, and Hughes le Gallais for their valuable books.
– Emanuela Notarbartolo di Sciara for sharing her family recipes.
– Vera and Briano Martinoni for sharing their wedding photographs.
– My mother-in-law, Giovanna, and to Lella de Girolamo for sharing their Venetian stories.
– Lucia and Matilde Zavagli for giving me a true education in the Venetian artists of the early years of the century.
– Roberta and Luigino Rossi for allowing me to discover their unusual collection of shoes representing the excellence of the Brenta.
– Viola and Vera Arrivabene, and bravo for working to ensure the continuation of the legendary *friulane* slippers, and to Perrine Renard for the photograph of them in a gondola.
– The descendants of Winnaretta Singer and to Bikem de Montebello for showing us around the Palazzo Polignac.
– Filippo, Benedetta, and Alessandro Gaggia for their welcome in the Palazzo Loredan dell'Ambasciatore.
– Martina Grimani for finding the original costume and jewelry her mother wore at the Beistegui Ball and for telling us about her father, the great artist Toni Luccarda.
– Licinio Garavaglia for admitting us into the very secret chinoiserie antechamber of the Palazzo Papadopoli and to Paolo Lorenzoni for allowing us into the mirror-lined bar of the Gritti Palace.
– Jacques Grange for making the Palazzo Falier a wonderful place.

– Shannon Bastianello for keeping the art of orientalism alive.
– Elizabeth Royer for her knowledge of the work of Alessandro Diaz de Santillana.
– Attilio Codognato and Alberto Nardi for giving us the opportunity to admire their archives of extraordinary jewelry.

Special thanks go to Alberto Torsello, the Maury brothers, and Mickey Riad and their team for allowing us to photograph the complete tables of Countess Elsie McNeil Lee Gozzi: without their help, the chapter dedicated to Mariano Fortuny would not have been the same. And thank you to Gabriella Belli, Chiara Squarcina, and Cristina Da Roit for working miracles in opening to us Mariano Fortuny's palazzo in Casa-Museo.
Thank you to the Bevilacqua workshops for perpetuating a centuries-old weaving tradition, and to the brothers Raffaele and Massimiliano Alajmo for giving Philippe Starck the opportunity to give it a contemporary twist.
Thank you to Stella Asta for her expertise in Olga Asta's shop and lace.
Thank you to Mario d'Alpaos from S.A.L.I.R. for explaining Venice and Murano glass to me, to the gallerists Alessandra and Alessandro Zoppi for revealing their treasures, and to the collectors Chahan Minassian and Richard Makin-Poole.
Congratulations to the artist Marcantonio Brandolini d'Adda for his new interpretations of glass, and thank you to Brandino Brandolini d'Adda for hosting us.
Thank you to Jane Da Mosto for allowing me to share the sense of humour of her beloved mother, Victoria Press.

The future of Venice lies in the expert hands of artists, architects, and interior designers:
Thank you to the sculptor Gigi Bon for doing us the honor of opening her studio and, most unusually, her home.
Thanks to Davide Battistin and Roger de Montebello for tirelessly painting Venice.
Thank you to Andrew Huston and Karole Vail for carrying on their family tradition.
Thank you to Marta Bastianello and her husband, Cesare Buzzi, for their passion and insight into ceramics.
Congratulations to Umberto Branchini for taking on the challenge of renovating and decorating historic palazzi.
Thank you to Inti and Cristina Ligabue for all their patronage and the exhibitions they have organized for the city.

I wish to thank all those who, anonymously or otherwise, have agreed to lift the veil on their daily lives and the interiors and exteriors of their homes.
I am thinking especially of Guillaume and Sylvie Roehrig, Gaby Wagner and Jean-Marie Degueldre, Maria Novella Benzoni, Susanne and Matteo Thun, Emanuela Schmeidler, Jérôme Zieseniss.
Thank you to the historians Roberto De Feo and Cristina Beltrami for their tireless answers to my many questions about Venetian artists and the history of the Biennale, and to France Thierard for her precious advice.
Thank you to Orsola Foscari for her personality, so typically Venetian, and her constant support.
Thank you to Mattia Aquila, whose vision has been indispensable over the months. This book could not have existed without his photographer's eye.
Thank you to Karine Huguenaud for her editorial support.

And finally, I am grateful to my family, children, parents, sisters, and brother, for their enthusiasm for my strange Venetian life.

PHOTOGRAPHIC CREDITS